# RIVERS *and* STREAMS

## A Guided Journey Through the Book of James

*For Individuals and Groups*

Karen Schexnayder

Rivers and Streams
A Guided Journey Through the Book of James
Karen Schexnayder

To contact the author: ksrands@yahoo.com

Published by:

Mary Ethel

Mary Ethel Eckard
Frisco, Texas

Library of Congress Catalog Number: 2022916509
ISBN (Print): 979-8-9868496-0-7
ISBN (E-book): 979-8-9868496-1-4

# CONTENTS

Preface .................................................................................................................... v

The Author .............................................................................................................. vii

How to Get the Most from this Devotional/Study ............................................ ix

1    The Testing of Faith ................................................................................... 1

2    The Purpose of Trials ............................................................................... 17

3    Wisdom ...................................................................................................... 33

4    Temptation ................................................................................................. 49

5    The Nature of God .................................................................................... 67

6    Doers of the Word .................................................................................... 85

7    Partiality .................................................................................................. 101

8    Faith and Works ...................................................................................... 119

9    Life and Death ........................................................................................ 137

10   The Power of the Tongue ....................................................................... 155

11   Two Kinds of Wisdom ............................................................................. 173

12   Ongoing Battle ........................................................................................ 189

13   Grace for the Win! ................................................................................. 207

14   Judging Others ........................................................................................ 225

15   Depend on the Lord ............................................................................... 241

16   Faith and Riches ..................................................................................... 257

17   Faith and Christ's Return ...................................................................... 275

18   Faith in Action ........................................................................................ 291

A Closing Word to the Reader ......................................................................... 307

Prayers from the Bible ...................................................................................... 309

Acknowledgements ............................................................................................ 311

Appendix A .......................................................................................................... 313

Notes .................................................................................................................... 315

# PREFACE

I can't remember a time when I didn't have a deep love for God. I was raised in a denomination that taught deep reverence for Him and I am so grateful. I was instructed in the knowledge of God; however, I knew something was missing. Thankfully, the Lord placed just the right godly women in my path who demonstrated more than just knowledge of God. They also had a deep and intimate relationship with Him.

At the age of twenty-one, I surrendered my whole heart to Jesus, and it has been an adventure ever since. Not long after entering this new relationship with the Lord, a wonderful Christian woman, Betty Taylor, took me under her wing and invited me to a Bible Study she was teaching. I signed up without knowing one thing about the Bible. I was terrified but jumped right into the deep end and fell in love with studying God's Word.

After participating in the Bible Study for a few years, I was invited to become a part of leadership, which involved leading and ministering to a small group of 15 women on a weekly basis. From there I became the Assistant Teaching Director, teaching when the Teaching Director (TD) was unavailable. When the TD stepped down, the mantle of leadership was handed to me. The Lord had been preparing me for this position for many years. My credentials can be found in 1 Corinthians 1:26-30,

> *"For you see your calling, brethren, that not many wise according to the flesh, not many mighty, not many noble, are called. But God has chosen the foolish things of the world to put to shame the wise, and God has chosen the weak things of the world to put to shame the things which are mighty; and the base things of the world and the things which are despised God has chosen, and the things which are not, to bring to nothing the things that are, that no flesh should glory in His presence. But of Him you are in Christ Jesus, who became for us wisdom from God—and righteousness and sanctification and redemption."*

As TD, I researched and prepared my own lectures for each study week, which I found exhilarating. Teaching God's Word filled me with joy. The history behind God's Word is very important, but if the application of His Word is not taught, it is only a history lesson. We need to know how to live according to God's Word. He gives us clear instructions for every area of life so we can live the abundant life He desires for us.

This devotional is designed to give the reader more than just a thought for the day from one verse. It is designed to cause the reader to ponder and meditate on God's Word. The Bible is its own best commentary. My opinion of the Word doesn't matter, but what God has to say does matter. The questions are written in such a way as to lead the reader to other scriptures which expound on and reinforce the scriptures in the book of James.

Romans 12:1-2 says,

> *"I beseech you therefore, brethren, by the mercies of God, that you present your bodies*
> *a living sacrifice, holy, acceptable to God, which is your reasonable service. And do*
> *not be conformed to this world, but be transformed by the renewing of your mind,*
> *that you may prove what is that good and acceptable and perfect will of God."*

The only way to renew our minds is to study and know God's Word. It has the power to convict, heal, and transform us into the image of Christ. The Word is the only offensive weapon provided by the armor of God, but a weapon is only useful if we are familiar with it and know how to use it. This devotional will help in all these areas as we ponder and meditate on the scriptures.

The title, Rivers and Streams, is derived from two scriptures. The first is Psalm 1, which says we will be like trees planted by the rivers of water, and Isaiah 43:19, which speaks of streams in the desert. It is my highest hope and prayer that the reader will be both established and refreshed in studying God's Word.

> *"Blessed is the man who walks not in the counsel of the ungodly, nor stands in the path*
> *of sinners, nor sits in the seat of the scornful; but his delight is in the law of the Lord, and in*
> *His law he meditates day and night. He shall be like a tree planted by the rivers of water, that*
> *brings forth its fruit in its season, whose leaf also shall not wither, and whatever he does shall prosper."*

Psalm 1:1-3 NKJV

> *"See, I am doing a new thing! Now it springs up; do you not perceive it?*
> *I am making a way in the wilderness and streams in the wasteland."*

Isaiah 43:19 NIV

Karen

Karen Schexnayder is a wife, mother, and grandmother. She is the former Teaching Director for Joy Bible Study and has participated in a disciplined Bible study for more than forty years. She has been a keynote speaker at several women's events, and several years of her teachings can be accessed through YouTube or on the Joy Bible Study Facebook page, https://www.facebook.com/joysetx

# HOW TO GET THE MOST FROM THIS DEVOTIONAL/STUDY

This devotional/study is uniquely designed for individual study and group settings. Both methods are effective for assisting in your quest for knowledge of God's Word and for growth in your Christian walk. I use several different translations of the Bible for study, research, and clarification but for the purpose of this study I used the NKJV version.

The Lord made it clear many years ago that salvation changes our destination, but the Word works the transformation in our lives as believers in Jesus Christ. The goal of every believer is to be conformed to the image of Christ. The only way this can occur is through the study and application of God's Word.

Each lesson has a devotion to read on the first day, followed by six days of questions for the reader to answer. There are one to five questions for each day depending on the scripture referenced. If there are only one or two questions, that is because they require more time to answer. The questions give the student an opportunity for a deeper dive into the Word and ultimately applying the truths learned in their own life experiences.

You will also find Journal pages after each lesson. Use these pages to record your thoughts, questions, answers, or revelations during your study for that day. Additional Journal pages can also be found at the back of the book.

Each day before opening God's Word, ask the Holy Spirit to lead and guide you into all truth. Ask Him to show you areas in your life that need to change. The Holy Spirit will also give you the courage to apply the Word so change can occur. Ask the Lord to cause His Word to become part of the fiber of your being so its words, thoughts, attitudes, and actions will become your own. In time you will realize how much His Word influences reactions as well.

The more time we spend in God's Word, the more we become like Him. It is an exciting, lifelong journey that will shape our beliefs and every part of who we are. What we believe is who we are. Who we are is what we do (behavior). Our actions reflect what we believe and Who we believe.

My prayer is for you to discover the rich treasure that is God's Word. May it become part of who you are and ultimately bless others as it manifests in your life.

WHAT MATTERS MOST IS THAT WE
*allow our trials*
TO ACCOMPLISH THEIR PURPOSES,
SO THAT WE MAY BECOME

*mature, complete
and lacking
nothing.*

# The Testing of Faith

*"My brethren, count it all joy when you fall into various trials, knowing that the testing of your faith produces patience. But let patience have its perfect work, that you may be perfect and complete, lacking nothing."*

James 1:2-4

Throughout life, we go through various trials. Trials are no respecter of persons. Trials transcend all barriers and are irrespective of gender, rank, prestige, race, creed, socio-economic status, age, degree of spiritual knowledge or strength, wealth, or poverty. Nothing can exempt us from nor prevent trials from coming into our lives and the testing of our faith through trials will impact our lives many times and in many ways.

For the believer, a good trial is never wasted! It is purposeful and will develop a better understanding of who God is to us, personally. His character is molded into us and is a means by which we can better serve the Lord in His kingdom. As His character is molded into us, we are transformed into the image of Jesus, and greater still is the fact that He is glorified in us as we humble ourselves under His mighty hand.

*"My brethren, count it all joy when you fall into various trials, knowing that the testing of your faith produces patience."*

James 1:2-3

James writes this as a command, not a suggestion. No one, when experiencing testing of faith through trials, can count it all joy unless their faith is in Christ, because it is the "joy of the Lord" that is our strength. It is knowing He is working everything out for our greater good and for His glory, which increases strength and endurance.

Tests of faith, or trials, are productive and beneficial. Patience is a product of the testing of our faith. If extremely hot fire is what brings forth the beauty from gold, then patience is the brilliance revealed by the fire of trials.

Patience: 1) The suffering of afflictions, pain, toil, calamity, provocation, or other evil, with a calm, unruffled temper; endurance without murmuring or fretfulness. 2) The act or quality of waiting long for justice or expected good, without discontent.[1]

Patience is not the end product of trials (testing). The completed work of patience is that we may become mature, complete, and lacking nothing.

Jesus was God's own begotten Son, yet He was not spared from pain and suffering. We should always be humbled by the fact that God has entrusted us with trials. He is betting we will pass the test. It's a safe bet for Him because He knows He will give us grace to see us through. In the end, what matters is that we allow the trial to accomplish its purpose, and thereby pass the test. In the midst of trials, let's learn to say with Jesus, "Father, glorify Your Name!"

## ADDITIONAL SCRIPTURE

1 Peter 1:6-7

1 Peter 5:10

John 12:28

### PRAYER

I thank you, Father, for strengthening my faith through trials.

Thank you for grace to sustain and see me through to the end.

Most of all, thank you for opportunities to become more like You.

Amen.

# Study Questions

**Read James 1:2-4**

1. How are we to consider the various trials we have in life?

2. What is produced from the trials?

# JOURNAL

Do the questions or scripture reading from today stir your spirit or emotions in any way?
Is there an area in your life or in your faith that needs a deeper look?

# Study Questions

**Read James 1:2-4**

1. Is patience beneficial?

2. Describe the evidence of patience in a believer.

# JOURNAL

Do the questions or scripture reading from today stir your spirit or emotions in any way?

Is there an area in your life or in your faith that needs a deeper look?

## Study Questions

**Read 1 Peter 1:5-7**

1. How are we preserved through trials?

2. Describe some of your own various trials.

3. In what ways has God preserved you through your trials?

# JOURNAL

Do the questions or scripture reading from today stir your spirit or emotions in any way?

Is there an area in your life or in your faith that needs a deeper look?

**Read 1 Peter 1:7**

1. How is genuine faith compared to gold and silver?

2. What is the longevity of faith compared to gold and silver?

# JOURNAL

Do the questions or scripture reading from today stir your spirit or emotions in any way?

Is there an area in your life or in your faith that needs a deeper look?

## Study Questions

**Read 1 Peter 1:7**

1. How is the intensity of trials described?

2. What kind of faith is revealed after such intense testing?

# JOURNAL

Do the questions or scripture reading from today stir your spirit or emotions in any way?

Is there an area in your life or in your faith that needs a deeper look?

# Study Questions

**Read John 12:28**

1. Write John 12:28.

2. What is the ultimate outcome of our trials?

# JOURNAL

Do the questions or scripture reading from today stir your spirit or emotions in any way?

Is there an area in your life or in your faith that needs a deeper look?

OUR GOD IS

*greater than*

THE
GREATEST TRIAL
WE COULD

*ever face.*

# The Purpose of Trials

*"My brethren, count it all joy when you fall into various trials, knowing that
the testing of your faith produces patience. But let patience have its perfect
work, that you may be perfect and complete, lacking nothing."*

James 1:2-4

Yes, trials have purpose! After enduring some very hard things in my life, I have learned that the purpose of trials is threefold, with many facets under each fold.

1. That we may know Him more intimately.
2. His character is molded into us – we become more like Him.
3. To further His kingdom – by comforting and strengthening others after we come through the trial.

Without exception, everything is purposeful! Nothing we endure is ever wasted in God's economy. We were created for the purpose of giving God glory, and we accomplish this by portraying Him in such a way as to give an accurate estimate of who He is in our lives. Every time we face difficulty, we have a choice to make. We can either demonstrate to the world that the enemy is greater and more powerful, or we can demonstrate that our God is greater and more powerful than anything that can touch our lives. Our God is greater than the greatest trial we could ever face.

More than any other thing, trials drive us to our knees and cause us to seek God through His Word. As we read, He reveals more and more about who He is to us, in us, and through us. During this process, we draw closer to Him, and He draws closer to us, creating a more intimate relationship. To know Him more fully and more intimately should be our quest. Trials are the tools He uses to instruct us. We learn more about His faithfulness, provision, protection, and love as we journey through these difficult times.

We become more like the people with whom we spend the most time. The same is true in spending time with God. Trials cause us to seek Him through His Word and, in doing so, we spend more time with Him. As we spend more time reading His Word, praying and listening to Him, His character is molded into us, and we become more like Him.

Trials were never meant to be an end in themselves. Trials are meant to benefit those who experience them, but also to benefit others in the kingdom who might be walking down a similar path. If we will offer the pain, suffering, and heartache back to God, He will provide opportunities for us to encourage others along the way.

In 1 Thessalonians 5:18, we are instructed to give thanks in all things. To offer thanksgiving in the middle of a trial is a sacrifice. We never feel like thanking God when the pain is so great, we think we won't survive. But as we are able to help others from our own experiences, we not only freely thank Him, but we offer praise because we understand the blessing it becomes to someone else!

## ADDITIONAL SCRIPTURE

1 Peter 1:6-9
1 Peter 5:10

### PRAYER

Father, as I triumph through my trials,
bring forth eternal dividends when I use what is learned through trial
to invest in the lives of others.
Amen.

# Study Questions

**Read 1 Peter 1:6-9**

1.  Does God control the duration of trials?

2.  Are trials necessary? Why or why not?

# JOURNAL

Do the questions or scripture reading from today stir your spirit or emotions in any way?
Is there an area in your life or in your faith that needs a deeper look?

# Study Questions

**Read 1 Peter 1:6-9**

1. When will the result of our testing be examined?

2. Who will examine the results?

# JOURNAL

Do the questions or scripture reading from today stir your spirit or emotions in any way?

Is there an area in your life or in your faith that needs a deeper look?

# Study Questions

**Read 1 Peter 1:8-9**

1. How is faith defined?

2. What is the end result of faith?

# JOURNAL

Do the questions or scripture reading from today stir your spirit or emotions in any way?
Is there an area in your life or in your faith that needs a deeper look?

# Study Questions

**Read 1 Peter 5:10**

1. How is God described?

2. Through whom do we access God's eternal glory?

# JOURNAL

Do the questions or scripture reading from today stir your spirit or emotions in any way?

Is there an area in your life or in your faith that needs a deeper look?

# Study Questions

**Read 1 Peter 5:10**

1. In your opinion, what do you believe impacts the duration of our suffering through trials?

2. List ways in which we benefit from the trial.

# JOURNAL

Do the questions or scripture reading from today stir your spirit or emotions in any way?

Is there an area in your life or in your faith that needs a deeper look?

## Study Questions

**Read James 1:2-4**

1. Can you describe a difficult trial through which God has brought you?

2. What did you experience emotionally during your trial?

3. Summarize ways in which you have grown in your faith through trials.

---

### PRAYER

Father, You work all things together for my good and Your glory.

Make Your name great through my trials.

Heal my emotions, for You are my healer!

Amen.

---

# JOURNAL

Do the questions or scripture reading from today stir your spirit or emotions in any way?

Is there an area in your life or in your faith that needs a deeper look?

WE ARE ALL

*equal in God's eyes.*

HE DOES NOT VIEW
PEOPLE IN TERMS OF

*financial means.*

# Wisdom

*"If any of you lacks wisdom, let him ask of God, who gives to all liberally and without reproach, and it will be given to him. But let him ask in faith, with no doubting, for he who doubts is like a wave of the sea driven and tossed by the wind. For let not that man suppose that he will receive anything from the Lord; he is a double-minded man, unstable in all his ways.*

*"Let the lowly brother glory in his exaltation, but the rich in his humiliation, because as a flower of the field he will pass away. For no sooner has the sun risen with a burning heat than it withers the grass; its flower falls, and its beautiful appearance perishes. So the rich man also will fade away in his pursuits.*

*"Blessed is the man who endures temptation; for when he has been approved, he will receive the crown of life which the Lord has promised to those who love Him."*

James 1:5-12

Many times, while going through difficult trials, we agonize over not knowing what to do or how to handle it. Trials come in many colors, shapes, and sizes. They can be relational, financial, physical, emotional, moral, or spiritual. If we are in Christ, it all boils down to a spiritual battle.

The battle ultimately comes down to one simple question:

### Are we going to trust God?

During these trials, James instructs us to go to the true source of wisdom – God!

In 2 Chronicles 20:1-12, Jehoshaphat gives us a perfect example. He found himself overwhelmed by his circumstances, he didn't know what to do, and he was afraid. What did Jehoshaphat purpose in his heart?

He determined in his heart to seek the Lord.

He fasted and prayed.

He maintained his focus on the Lord.

He believed God would hear and answer his prayers.

The Word tells us that God will give us wisdom liberally, generously, abundantly, and without reproach. He doesn't fuss at us or point out our faults and failings or reasons we are undeserving. But there is one hitch – we must ask, believing by faith that He will give us the wisdom for which we have asked. God compares doubt with instability and goes on to say we are like waves of the sea tossed to and fro. This tossing means we are not anchored or grounded, and God answers prayers of faith, not doubt.

We are all equal in God's eyes. He does not view people in terms of financial means. Yet, in our worldly way of thinking, we tend to look down on those of lesser financial means, while we elevate those who are wealthy. We treat them differently. One weekend, on our wedding anniversary, a dear friend loaned us his Jaguar convertible. Everywhere we went, people assumed we had money and extended greater privilege and courtesy than if we had shown up in our Honda. These verses are not an indictment of the rich, but rather show that trials are a great equalizer. Neither poverty nor wealth excludes us from trials; we are all equal in God's eyes. We all access grace and wisdom from the same source – GOD! That is why He says the poor man is exalted and the rich brought low. We are all equal in God's eyes.

All the things on which we place value in this world – wealth, position, and fame – are just temporal and will not last. When we allow the trial to accomplish its purpose and we pass the test, we secure eternal treasures given to those who love Him.

## ADDITIONAL SCRIPTURE

2 Chronicles 20:3, 6-12

Jeremiah 29:11-13

John 12:28

## PRAYER

Father,

As I go through trials, help me seek Your wisdom first.

The wisdom that comes from above.

As I look to You, please guide my every step and glorify Your name in all I do.

Amen.

## Study Questions

**Read James 1:5**

1. What do we sometimes lack when going through difficult times?

2. Who should we ask to supply us?

3. How is this given? Is there a limit?

# JOURNAL

Do the questions or scripture reading from today stir your spirit or emotions in any way?

Is there an area in your life or in your faith that needs a deeper look?

## Study Questions

**Read James 1:6-8**

1.  How should we ask for this supply? What should be excluded when we ask?

2.  What is a doubting person compared to?

3.  What kind of person will not receive from the Lord? How is this person characterized in verse 8?

4.  Define doubleminded. Define unstable.

5.  Does this affect everything we do?

# JOURNAL

Do the questions or scripture reading from today stir your spirit or emotions in any way?

Is there an area in your life or in your faith that needs a deeper look?

## Study Questions

**Read 2 Chronicles 20:3**

1. What was Jehoshaphat's emotional state? What did he determine to do? What extra measure did he take when seeking the Lord?

**Read 2 Chronicles 20:6-12**

2. Based on the scripture from verses 6-7, write the phrases giving God praise and list God's previous accomplishments.

3. In verse 9, what is Jehoshaphat confident God will do? Where is Jehoshaphat's focus?

4. Describe Jehoshaphat's petition to God found in verses 10-12.

# JOURNAL

Do the questions or scripture reading from today stir your spirit or emotions in any way?

Is there an area in your life or in your faith that needs a deeper look?

## Study Questions

**Read Jeremiah 29:11-13**

1. What does verse 11 say about God's plans for believers?

2. What does He promise when we pray?

3. What does He promise when we seek Him?

4. How should we seek Him?

# JOURNAL

Do the questions or scripture reading from today stir your spirit or emotions in any way?

Is there an area in your life or in your faith that needs a deeper look?

# Study Questions

**Read James 1:9-11**

1. What do these verses say about those from different socio-economic status?

2. How long does wealth last?

3. In what way do trials equalize people?

4. How does God view all people?

# JOURNAL

Do the questions or scripture reading from today stir your spirit or emotions in any way?

Is there an area in your life or in your faith that needs a deeper look?

## DAY 6
## Study Questions

**Read James 1:12**

1.  How does this describe one who endures temptation?

2.  When approved, what will this one receive from the Lord?

3.  To whom is this promise given?

**Read John 12:28**

4.  When going through trials, what should we declare?

---

### PERSONAL

How does this lesson speak to your heart in the trials
you are currently walking through?

---

### PRAYER

Let's follow the example of Jesus when going through trials.
Let His prayer be our prayer.
"Father, glorify Your name!"

# JOURNAL

Do the questions or scripture reading from today stir your spirit or emotions in any way?

Is there an area in your life or in your faith that needs a deeper look?

THERE IS

*absolutely no circumstance*

IN WHICH GOD WOULD TEMPT
US TO SIN AGAINST HIM.

INSTEAD, HE PROVIDES A
WAY OF ESCAPE IF WE
SIMPLY PAUSE AND LOOK TO

*Him for help.*

# Temptation

*"Let no one say when he is tempted, "I am tempted by God"; for God cannot be tempted by evil, nor does He Himself tempt anyone. But each one is tempted when he is drawn away by his own desires and enticed. Then, when desire has conceived, it gives birth to sin; and sin, when it is full-grown, brings forth death. Do not be deceived, my beloved brethren."*

James 1:13-16

Trials are things that blow through our lives without warning! We have no control over their timing, duration, or devastation. However, temptation is quite different. Temptation is something to which we choose to open the door and allow into our lives.

The other day, a young girl knocked on my door. When I opened the door, she asked if I wanted to buy a chocolate candy bar. Well of course I said YES, and then justified it with the fact that I was "helping" her out!

That is what happens when Satan comes knocking. We choose to open the door. He offers something that will gratify our fleshly desires. Then we choose to buy into the lie he is selling. Temptation is always aimed at indulging and satisfying our fleshly desires.

Eve was tempted in the garden of Eden by Satan. He appealed to the lust of the eyes by offering something pleasing to her senses -- the fruit. Next, he appealed to the lust of the flesh by offering something to satisfy her hunger. Then he appealed to the pride of life -- she would be wise like God. After falling for his lies, she then offered the same temptation to her husband. We are still experiencing the domino effect of their sin.

There is absolutely no circumstance in which God would tempt us to sin against Him. Instead, He provides a way of escape for us if we simply pause and look to Him for help. Temptation is a design of the enemy to test our loyalty to God. Are we going to follow God and His Word, or are we going to be led astray and follow the one who wants to destroy us and our witness for God? God allows trials that strengthen our faith, but He is in no way responsible for our being tempted or enticed to sin against Him. Temptation to sin is the sole work of the enemy. God is holy and without the capacity to sin. God is light; in Him, there is no darkness. Temptation is the work of Satan who is darkness and dwells in darkness.

Our problem is not external, but internal. It is our own heart and mind that gets us into trouble. In our human anatomy, conception occurs when an egg and sperm unite to become one. The result is the birth of a child. Spiritually speaking, when fleshly desire, which begins in our mind, becomes one with temptation, sin is birthed. If sin is allowed to grow, it will result in death; death of dreams, plans, relationships, and sometimes even physical death.

Temptation, by itself, has no effect on us until we become partners with it. Once we partner with temptation, it is progressive. We entertain it in our minds. We are drawn to it by the lust of our eyes, the lust of our flesh, and the pride of life; then we act on it. Once we act on it, we are guilty of sin. Sin is also progressive. There is a familiar saying that goes like this:

Sow a thought; reap an action.
Sow an action; reap a habit.
Sow a habit; reap a lifestyle.

We cannot keep thoughts from entering our minds any more than we can keep a bird from flying over our heads. However, we can prevent the bird from building a nest in our hair, and we can prevent the temptation from becoming sin. Once sin enters, before we know it, sin controls us, and we are no longer in charge.

Fishermen use various kinds of bait to entice different kinds of fish. Some of the baits are pretty, shiny, wiggly, spinners, and some are fresh, such as worms, shrimp, or minnows. The one thing these baits have in common is they are attached to a concealed sharp hook. When the fish is out to satisfy its desires, he is enticed by the bait, then he swallows the bait, and the hook is set.

Satan is the fisherman and worldly pleasures are the bait. Out of a longing to fulfill our own desires, we take his bait, and he sets the hook. Just like the fish, we are deceived by what appears to be something that would satisfy, only to find out it is a death trap. The only way to guard against the deception Satan uses to lure us into temptation is to set our minds on things above.

Daily time spent in the Word of God will help keep us aware of the tactics of the enemy. We need to maintain a focus of pleasing God and not ourselves. It is imperative to anchor ourselves in the Word. The Truth will set us free!

# ADDITIONAL SCRIPTURE

Genesis 3:6

1 Corinthians 10:1

## PRAYER

Father, help me set my mind and heart on things above.
Guard me from the schemes and deception of the enemy.
Let the thoughts of my mind and the intentions of
my heart be acceptable to you, Lord.

Amen.

# Study Questions

**Read James 1:13-16**

1.  What do some people say when temptation comes their way?

2.  Can God be tempted?

3.  Does God tempt people?

# JOURNAL

Do the questions or scripture reading from today stir your spirit or emotions in any way?

Is there an area in your life or in your faith that needs a deeper look?

# *Study Questions*

**Read James 1:13-16**

1. When is a person tempted?

2. List some areas in your life that could be vulnerable to temptation.

# JOURNAL

Do the questions or scripture reading from today stir your spirit or emotions in any way?

Is there an area in your life or in your faith that needs a deeper look?

# DAY 3
## Study Questions

**Read James 1:13-16**

1. Name the partner of desire, found in verse 14. What happens when these two unite?

2. Name the "baby" that comes when desire has conceived.

3. What is brought forth when this "baby" is fully mature?

4. Does this refer to physical, spiritual, or both?

# JOURNAL

Do the questions or scripture reading from today stir your spirit or emotions in any way?

Is there an area in your life or in your faith that needs a deeper look?

## Study Questions

**Read James 1:16**

1. What are we commanded?

2. How can we guard against deception?

# JOURNAL

Do the questions or scripture reading from today stir your spirit or emotions in any way?

Is there an area in your life or in your faith that needs a deeper look?

# Study Questions

**Read Genesis 3:6**

1. Describe the progression of sin from start to finish.

2. Does our sin affect us only?

# JOURNAL

Do the questions or scripture reading from today stir your spirit or emotions in any way?

Is there an area in your life or in your faith that needs a deeper look?

## Study Questions

**Read 1 Corinthians 10:13**

1. Is temptation unique to any one individual?

2. Will God allow us to be tempted beyond what we are able to withstand?

3. How does God provide for us when we are overtaken by temptation?

# JOURNAL

Do the questions or scripture reading from today stir your spirit or emotions in any way?

Is there an area in your life or in your faith that needs a deeper look?

A PERSON WHO RULES THEIR SPIRIT IS BETTER THAN HE WHO TAKES A CITY.

There is power in controlling the tongue.

# The Nature of God

*"Every good gift and every perfect gift is from above, and comes down from the Father of lights, with whom there is no variation or shadow of turning. Of His own will, He brought us forth by the word of truth, that we might be a kind of first fruits of His creatures.*

*"So then, my beloved brethren, let every man be swift to hear, slow to speak, slow to wrath; for the wrath of man does not produce the righteousness of God.*

*"Therefore lay aside all filthiness and overflow of wickedness, and receive with meekness the implanted word, which is able to save your souls.*

*"Be ye doers of the word, and not hearers only, deceiving yourselves."*

James 1:17-22

Our natural tendency toward sin and Satan's constant attempts to lure us into sin are in stark contrast to the nature of God.

**God's nature:**
Holy, pure, just, loving, merciful; He is light, truth, compassion, and life.

**Father of lights**:
This is the Hebrew description or name for God, which declares Him as Creator of lights – sun, moon, stars. But He is also the Father of all believers, whom the Word also calls lights. In Matthew 5:14-16, Jesus speaks to believers, and He calls us "lights."

God is light and He is good. He is the giver of every good and perfect gift. All these good things emanate from Him because they flow from His very nature. God is the same yesterday, today, and forever. He is unchanging; therefore, it is not possible for anything but good to come from Him.

What does He give? He gave His only begotten Son, Jesus. Through faith in Jesus, we access many gifts from God. We receive His Holy Spirit, His power, His peace, His grace, and eternal life, to name a few.

God chose to birth us into His kingdom by the word of truth, which is the gospel. We are washed clean and regenerated by the Word of God. It is God's purpose for us to become a kind of first fruits. Think about it: when we give our lives to Christ, we are the first fruit of a spiritual crop that will follow as we impact the lives of others for Christ.

If we are to be effective in bringing others to Christ, we must learn a few basic principles and incorporate them into our lives. The Word tells us we must be swift to hear, slow to speak, slow to wrath; for the wrath of man does not produce the righteousness of God.

**Swift to hear**: Just as we tune into a radio station, we must tune our ears to hear what God has to say. We must be quick to hear what His Word is speaking into our lives. His Word gives us rules for living, uncovers errors in our thinking and behavior, corrects the error, and teaches us how to proceed in righteousness.

**Slow to speak**: God's Word is clear on this. Those who are hasty in their words are likened to a fool. It tells us that even fools, when they hold their peace, are counted as wise. Let us ask the Lord to set a watch over our mouths and keep the door of our lips. Let's ask the Lord to teach us to be quiet. (Just so you know, this writer is still working on perfecting this!)

**Slow to wrath**: There is nothing righteous about a hot-tempered person. Our anger is counter-productive to accomplishing the righteousness of God. Proverbs tells us that a quick-tempered man acts foolishly. The antithesis of a quick temper would be a person who is slow to anger. The Word tells us that a man who is slow to anger is better than the mighty. A person who rules their spirit is better than he who takes a city. There is power in controlling our tongue.

Careless words and unrighteous anger produce evil and moral corruption, as well as attitudes contrary to the Word and work of God. We must lay aside these destructive attitudes and actions, which become barriers to hearing and doing the Word of God. We need to receive, with humility, the Word God plants in our hearts as we read and study it so we will not be deceived. To receive the Word of God, we must allow it to become part of the very fiber of our being. We must be diligent to maintain both tilled and fertile soil in our hearts so the Word can take root and become fruitful in our lives.

# ADDITIONAL SCRIPTURE

Proverbs 14:17

Proverbs 16:32

Proverbs 17:28

Proverbs 29:20

Malachi 3:6

Colossians 3:8-9, 12-14

2 Timothy 3:16-17

Hebrews 13:8

## Study Questions

**Read James 1:17-21**

1. How is the Father described?

2. Identify the instructions to believers.

3. What doesn't the wrath of man produce?

4. List the things we are to lay aside. What are we to receive and what should be our attitude in receiving?

**Read Malachi 3:6**

5. What specific attribute of God is listed?

Do the questions or scripture reading from today stir your spirit or emotions in any way?

Is there an area in your life or in your faith that needs a deeper look?

## Study Questions

**Read 2 Timothy 3:16-17**

1. How is scripture given?

2. List the ways in which scripture is beneficial.

3. Describe the end goal of scripture.

# JOURNAL

Do the questions or scripture reading from today stir your spirit or emotions in any way?

Is there an area in your life or in your faith that needs a deeper look?

## Study Questions

**Read Proverbs 17:28**

1.  Name two ways a "fool" is described when he holds his tongue.

**Read Proverbs 29:20**

2.  What does this say about a person who is hasty in his words?

---

### PRAYER

Father, set a watch over my mouth and keep the door of my lips.

Teach me to be slow to speak and quick to listen.

Help me learn to be quiet.

Amen.

---

Do the questions or scripture reading from today stir your spirit or emotions in any way?

Is there an area in your life or in your faith that needs a deeper look?

# Study Questions

**Read Proverbs 14:17**

1. How is the behavior of a quick-tempered person described?

2. Describe a situation in which you feel you acted foolishly because of losing your temper.

**Read Proverbs 16:32**

3. What does the Bible say about someone who is slow to anger?

4. Describe a situation in which you experienced the benefits of controlling your anger.

# JOURNAL

Do the questions or scripture reading from today stir your spirit or emotions in any way?

Is there an area in your life or in your faith that needs a deeper look?

## Study Questions

**Read Colossians 3:8-9**

1.   List the behaviors associated with our old nature.

2.   Is effort required to eliminate these from our lives, or does it happen automatically?

**Read Colossians 3:12-17**

3.   List the behaviors that should characterize those who have a new nature in Christ Jesus.

---

**PERSONAL**

Do you see things in yourself that need to change? Explain

---

# JOURNAL

Do the questions or scripture reading from today stir your spirit or emotions in any way?

Is there an area in your life or in your faith that needs a deeper look?

## DAY 6
## Study Questions

**Read James 1:22**

1. Is it enough to hear or know the Word of God?


2. What should naturally follow after hearing the Word?


3. If we have knowledge of God's Word but do not obey, what does the Word say we are doing to ourselves?

# JOURNAL

Do the questions or scripture reading from today stir your spirit or emotions in any way?

Is there an area in your life or in your faith that needs a deeper look?

THE GOAL OF SPENDING TIME IN GOD'S WORD IS TO, OF COURSE, *know God more intimately.*

SALVATION CHANGES OUR DESTINATION, *the Word works the transformation.*

# Doers of the Word

*"But be doers of the word, and not hearers only, deceiving yourselves. For if anyone is a hearer of the word and not a doer, he is like a man observing his natural face in a mirror; for he observes himself, goes away, and immediately forgets what kind of man he was. But he who looks into the perfect law of liberty and continues in it and is not a forgetful hearer but a doer of the word, this one will be blessed in what he does.*

*"If anyone among you thinks he is religious and does not bridle his tongue but deceives his own heart, this one's religion is useless. Pure and undefiled religion before God and the Father is this: to visit orphans and widows in their trouble, and to keep oneself unspotted from the world."*

James 1:22-27

It is not enough to hear or even comprehend the Word. Unless we become doers of the Word by putting it into the practice of our daily lives, it will not be completed in us. We deceive ourselves if we believe it is only for the purpose of head knowledge. This was never God's intent in giving His Word. Head knowledge only serves to puff us up, making us prideful and arrogant. It is only in applying the Word to our daily lives that the Word is completed in us.

Failing to apply God's Word as we read it is the same as looking into a mirror and realizing a need to make corrections yet walking away from the mirror and dismissing what has been revealed. Women are notorious for checking themselves in the mirror to see if their clothes are in the proper place, and checking their make-up, teeth, and noses. Sometimes we even use each other to see if anything needs fixing; you can bet the necessary adjustments will be made.

What good does it do to read God's Word, have it reveal changes that need to be made, yet close it, walk away, and ignore what has been revealed? That's about as ridiculous as not getting the food out of our teeth after someone has told us it's there. Yet, through the mirror of His Word, God reveals changes we need to make, but we walk away ignoring what God has revealed.

God promises we will be blessed in what we do if we will read and DO His Word. With a guarantee like that, why would we dismiss what He reveals? As we read His Word, we should ask Him to reveal us to ourselves. We should also ask Him to show us how to make all the needed corrections. The goal in spending time in God's Word is to, of course, know God more intimately, but also to conform to the image of Jesus. Salvation changes our destination, but the Word works the transformation. We desire more than fire insurance[2] when we come to Christ in faith. Our deep desire is to become like Him; to have His thoughts, His ways, His actions, and more importantly, His reactions. This can only be accomplished through the study of and meditation on the Word, which should result in applying His teachings to our lives. (To learn more about the Plan of Salvation and how to receive the gift of forgiveness, see Appendix A in the back of the book.)

As we allow His Word to change us and make us more like Him, there will be evidence of the transformation. The natural effect of the Word is to change our hearts. Whatever fills our hearts will flow freely from our mouths. If we simply go to church and fulfill religious obligations while neglecting to incorporate His Word into our lives, our speech will reveal it. Spending time in the Word does more than make us religious, it develops a deep relationship with God. The Word is His love letter to us, which reveals His heart and who He is; communication is key to any relationship. The Word will change our desires to reflect God's desires. More and more we will have a different mindset. Our desire will truly be to care for those in need and to guard ourselves against the perspective and influence of the world.

## ADDITIONAL SCRIPTURE

Luke 6:45

1 John 2:15-16

## PRAYER

Father, teach me to seek You in Your Word.

Make me more like You.

Reveal the things I need to change in my life, and give

me the courage to make those changes.

Teach me to apply what I learn so others will have

an accurate picture of who You are.

Amen.

## Study Questions

**Read James 1:22**

1. Identify the exhortation (exhortation: the act of strongly encouraging or trying to persuade someone to do something.)[3]

2. What does it mean to be a doer of the Word?

3. What do we do to ourselves as a result of not heeding the exhortation?

# JOURNAL

Do the questions or scripture reading from today stir your spirit or emotions in any way?

Is there an area in your life or in your faith that needs a deeper look?

## Study Questions

**Read James 1:23-24**

1. What does the Word say we are like when we hear the Word but don't walk according to the Word?

2. What is the purpose of looking in a mirror?

3. In what ways is not applying and doing God's Word the same as seeing yourself in a mirror and just walking away without making the necessary adjustments?

# JOURNAL

Do the questions or scripture reading from today stir your spirit or emotions in any way?

Is there an area in your life or in your faith that needs a deeper look?

# Study Questions

**Read James 1:25**

1. How is God's Word described?

2. What are we instructed to do?

3. What promise is given?

# JOURNAL

Do the questions or scripture reading from today stir your spirit or emotions in any way?

Is there an area in your life or in your faith that needs a deeper look?

## Study Questions

**Read James 1:26-27**

1. Describe the correlation between genuine faith in God and the use of our words.


2. How is true faith in God defined?


3. List ways in which you can minister in these areas.


4. What does it mean to keep ourselves unspotted from the world?

# JOURNAL

Do the questions or scripture reading from today stir your spirit or emotions in any way?

Is there an area in your life or in your faith that needs a deeper look?

# *Study Questions*

**Read Luke 6:45**

1. Where do our deeds and words originate?

2. List ways in which we can guard our hearts.

3. Name the two ways man is described.

# JOURNAL

Do the questions or scripture reading from today stir your spirit or emotions in any way?

Is there an area in your life or in your faith that needs a deeper look?

## DAY 6
### Study Questions

**Read 1 John 2:15-16**

1. What are we commanded not to love?




2. List some things this would include.




3. What is true about those who love the world?

# JOURNAL

Do the questions or scripture reading from today stir your spirit or emotions in any way?

Is there an area in your life or in your faith that needs a deeper look?

JESUS IS ABOUT

*meeting needs,*

NOT MEASURING
CREDENTIALS.

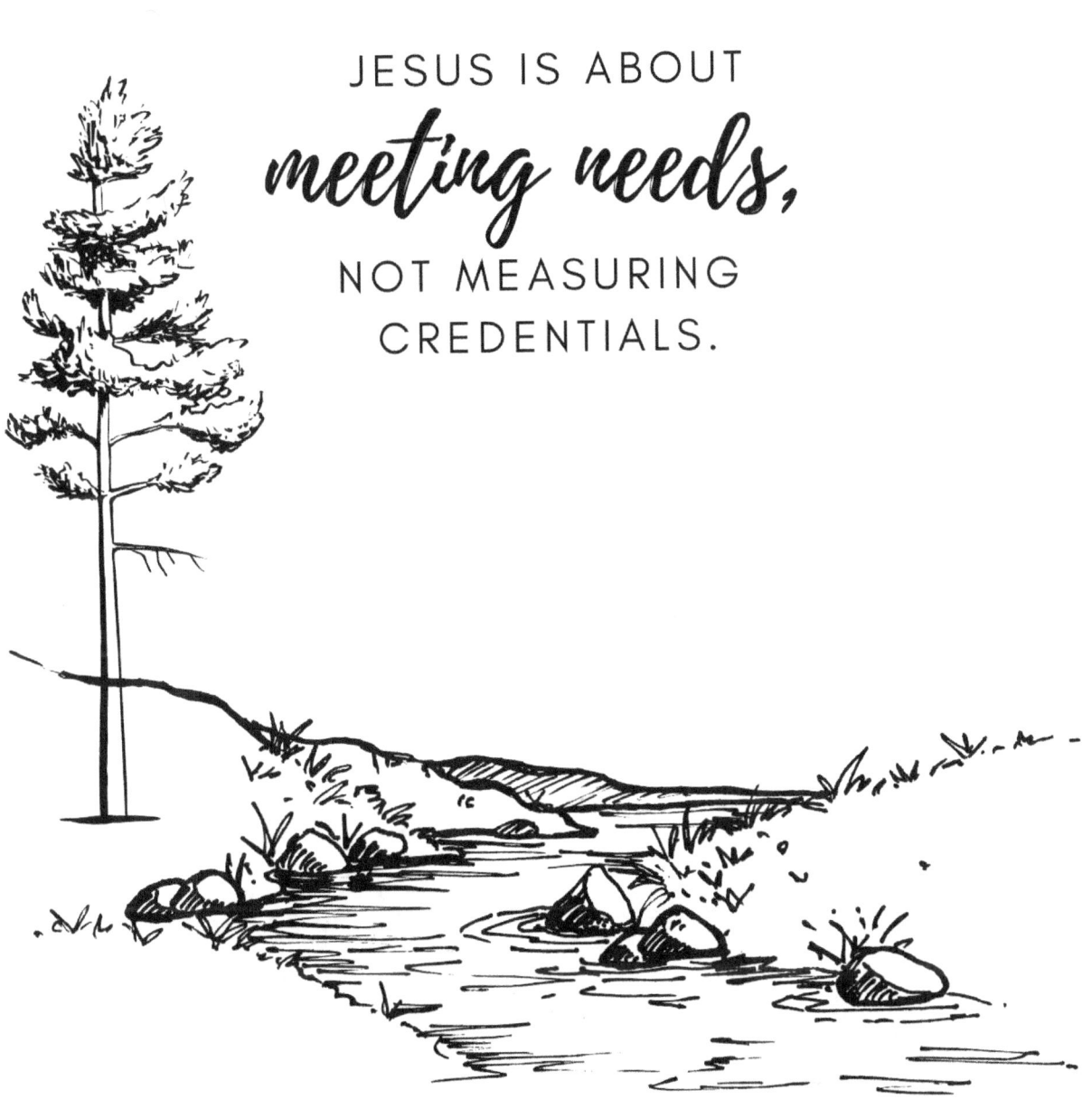

# Partiality

*"My brethren, do not hold the faith of our Lord Jesus Christ, the Lord of glory, with partiality. For if there should come into your assembly a man with gold rings, in fine apparel, and there should also come in a poor man in filthy clothes, and you pay attention to the one wearing the fine clothes and say to him, 'You sit here in a good place,' and say to the poor man, 'You stand there,' or, 'Sit here at my footstool,' have you not shown partiality among yourselves, and become judges with evil thoughts?*

*"Listen, my beloved brethren: Has God not chosen the poor of this world to be rich in faith and heirs of the kingdom which He promised to those who love Him? But you have dishonored the poor man. Do not the rich oppress you and drag you into the courts? Do they not blaspheme that noble name by which you are called?*

*"If you really fulfill the royal law according to the Scripture, 'You shall love your neighbor as yourself,' you do well; but if you show partiality, you commit sin, and are convicted by the law as transgressors. For whoever shall keep the whole law, and yet stumble in one point, he is guilty of all. For He who said, 'Do not commit adultery,' also said, 'Do not murder.' Now if you do not commit adultery, but you do murder, you have become a transgressor of the law. So speak and so do as those who will be judged by the law of liberty. For judgment is without mercy to the one who has shown no mercy. Mercy triumphs over judgment."*

James 2:1-13

In our culture, there are many ways in which we show partiality. We tend to judge the value of someone based on outward appearance -- clothes, cars, houses, position, power, and prestige are just a few of the ways we judge a person's worth. We treat people according to the measure of value we assign them according to the resume' listed above. For instance, if someone famous or wealthy was coming to our house, we would prepare and offer only the best. However, if someone we deem less-desirable shows up at our door, we might not even invite them in for a cool cup of water. Of course, in this day and time, we must be discerning about whom we invite into our home, but the principle stands. We should treat all people as though they have great worth.

If we are going to reflect Christ accurately, we need to find God's perspective on the matter. Impartiality is one of the attributes of God. He is above all and is the only righteous judge. He alone executes justice. He considers all believers to be equal in His sight, and more than that, He says we are joint heirs with Jesus Christ. Wisdom is also an attribute of God, and according to the Word, impartiality is a characteristic of wisdom.

Impartiality breaks down barriers and removes hindrances to the furthering of the kingdom of God. The world sizes people up and extends favor based on outward appearance or accomplishments. This is not so with God. He often chooses the least likely, the ones no one else would choose, in order to accomplish His purpose. The Word tells us that the more unqualified we are, the more obvious it is God working through us. While we tend to focus on pedigree in considering the value of others, God examines the heart. The lineage of Jesus Christ confirms this truth.

In the lineage of Christ, we find:

David – an adulterer and murderer

Tamar – a victim of incest and rape

Ruth – she was not even Jewish

Solomon – the son of David and Bathsheba with whom David committed adultery

Rahab – a non-Jew and a harlot

These are just some of the skeletons in Jesus' closet, yet He is Messiah, King of Kings and Lord of Lords. His name is above all names, and all will bow to Him. By example, God demonstrates there is nothing He cannot overcome in order to use us for His kingdom purposes. The only thing that hinders His purpose for us is an unbelieving heart. In John 3:16, God extends a universal, all-inclusive invitation to accept His gift of salvation.

The ministry of Jesus went hand-in-hand with His mission. Think about it: if Jesus, who is creator, sustainer, and owner of all, humbled Himself and came in human form to die a cruel death for us, who are we to distinguish between people and assess their value or worth? Jesus' ministry was to the outcasts in this world: a harlot, leper, blind beggar, cripple, and adulterer, to name a few, and such were some of us. Jesus is about meeting needs, not measuring credentials.

If we are to truly reflect Christ, we need to start by extending the same compassionate treatment to all people. In John 13:34, Jesus says we are to love others as He has loved us. By His example, we are to love others sacrificially. We are to put the needs of others above our own and demonstrate unconditional love to all.

## ADDITIONAL SCRIPTURE

Deuteronomy 1:17, 10:17

2 Chronicles 19:5-7

Proverbs 24:23

John 3:16

John 13:34

Acts 10:34-35

## PRAYER

Lord, I am so grateful You have given me everything I need
to accomplish all You require of me, as Your child.
I have the capacity to love all others because You, Lord, love them through me.

Amen.

## *Study Questions*

**Read James 2:1-4**

1. How is Jesus described?

2. What instruction is given to Christians?

3. Describe the two classes of people represented.

4. How do we show partiality? When we show partiality, how does this scripture describe us?

# JOURNAL

Do the questions or scripture reading from today stir your spirit or emotions in any way?

Is there an area in your life or in your faith that needs a deeper look?

# DAY 2
## Study Questions

**Read James 2:5-13**

1. According to verse 5, who has God chosen?

2. Describe the blessings assured to those chosen.

3. The rich are accused of what three things?

4. In what way do we fulfill the law?

5. What is showing partiality called? What is the consequence of showing partiality? What does this say about those who keep the whole law but stumble in one point?

---

### CHALLENGE

Why does mercy triumph over judgment?
Explain your answer in the Journal section.

---

# JOURNAL

Do the questions or scripture reading from today stir your spirit or emotions in any way?

Is there an area in your life or in your faith that needs a deeper look?

## Study Questions

**Read Deuteronomy 1:17**

**Read Deuteronomy 10:17**

1. What are the guidelines for judgment?

2. Who is ultimately the judge?

3. List the qualities of a just judge.

# JOURNAL

Do the questions or scripture reading from today stir your spirit or emotions in any way?

Is there an area in your life or in your faith that needs a deeper look?

## Study Questions

**Read 2 Chronicles 19:5-7**

1.  What was Jehoshaphat's first action to bring order to the kingdom?

2.  What warning did he give to the judges?

3.  List the guidelines for the judges.

# JOURNAL

Do the questions or scripture reading from today stir your spirit or emotions in any way?

Is there an area in your life or in your faith that needs a deeper look?

# Study Questions

**Read Proverbs 24:23**

1.  Describe a characteristic of the wise.

2.  Have you ever been guilty of showing partiality? Explain.

3.  How can we guard against showing partiality?

# JOURNAL

Do the questions or scripture reading from today stir your spirit or emotions in any way?

Is there an area in your life or in your faith that needs a deeper look?

## Study Questions

**Read Acts 10:34-35**

1.  What does Peter discover about God?

2.  Is anyone excluded?

3.  What are the conditions for acceptance by God?

4.  What does it mean to "work" righteousness?

# JOURNAL

Do the questions or scripture reading from today stir your spirit or emotions in any way?

Is there an area in your life or in your faith that needs a deeper look?

# God's work is an inside job.

HE CHANGES OUR HEARTS WHEN WE TRULY REPENT AND BELIEVE IN JESUS.

THE WORK HE ACCOMPLISHES ON THE INSIDE ALWAYS MANIFESTS ITSELF IN OUR *outward actions.*

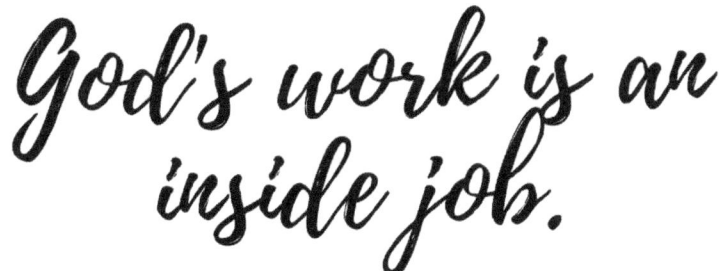

# Faith and Works

*"What does it profit, my brethren, if someone says he has faith but does not have works? Can faith save him? If a brother or sister is naked and destitute of daily food, and one of you says to them, 'Depart in peace, be warm and filled,' but you do not give them the things which are needed for the body, what does it profit? Thus also faith by itself, if it does not have works, is dead.*

*"But someone will say, 'You have faith, and I have works.' Show me your faith without your works, and I will show you my faith by my works."*

James 2:14-18

Genuine faith in Christ will be demonstrated by our works. Works alone cannot save us; however, genuine faith will manifest itself outwardly through the things we do (works). If someone says they have faith and do not have any works to prove their faith, then the genuineness of that faith is brought into question.

Anyone who says they have faith in Christ but turns their back, withholding compassion from someone in need, has a faith that is in word only. The heart has not been engaged in this kind of faith. Once we have repented and emptied ourselves before God, the regenerate heart longs to be used by God to accomplish His work. We cannot work our way to heaven; we cannot be "good" enough to get there. Neither can we verbalize faith yet be devoid of any outward demonstration of the change that should have occurred inside. God's work is an inside job. He changes our hearts when we truly repent and believe in Jesus. The work He accomplishes on the inside always manifests itself in our outward actions. We become doers of the Word.

The concept of faith and works is difficult to understand. I was pondering these truths and asked God to give me an illustration that would depict the correlation between faith and works. It was a cool fall day, and I was sitting outside in our courtyard enjoying God's Word and the beauty of His creation when He gave me the perfect analogy.

Our area had suffered severe drought during the summer, and I was scanning the flower beds to assess the damage to my plants. Even though I had watered every other day during the summer, we still lost several plants, including some azalea bushes. The Lord taught me the correlation between faith and works through those dead azalea bushes.

The dead azalea bush is like faith without works. I can tell you it is an azalea bush, but there is nothing to prove it. This bush had no foliage, no flowers, and no hope of having any because it was dead. It was totally unrecognizable as an azalea bush. I can work miracles with a hot glue gun and silk flowers, gluing them to the branches to make it look as though it were a living azalea bush, but upon close examination you would be able to see it is a facade.

The Pharisees and Sadducees, who fulfilled all the religious requirements, may have looked good on the outside, but closer examination would reveal no life in Christ -- dead faith. Their works were like those silk flowers!

The same analogy helps to explain faith without works. I can tell you I have faith, but like that dead azalea bush without real leaves or real flowers, how can you know for sure that I have faith? Genuine faith is proven or demonstrated by the quality of works done for the kingdom and will always bring glory and honor to God.

Man looks on the outward appearance, but God examines the heart. What we believe defines who we are, and who we are determines what we do (our behavior). The things we manipulate and make happen and the things we do for show are not the quality works spoken of here. The quality works are those prepared for us by God, the things He leads us into and the opportunities He presents for us. However, obedience is key to exhibiting quality works. We must be doers of His Word and not hearers only. This kind of work will always be characterized by compassion with the goal of making a difference in someone else's life. These works will bring glory, honor, and praise to God.

Do you want to bring glory, honor, and praise to God? Ask Him to show you the works He has prepared for you. You will be amazed what God can accomplish through a heart that is willing and available.

# ADDITIONAL SCRIPTURE

Ephesians 2:8-10

Titus 3:8

1 John 3:17

## PRAYER

Father, strip me of everything that does not honor You.

Show me the works You have prepared for me so all may know my faith is in You.

Let everything I think, say, and do be acceptable in Your sight.

Amen.

## Study Questions

**Read James 2:14-16**

1. If faith is in word only, can that kind of faith save us?

2. Describe the basic needs listed.

3. Define faith that is in word only.

4. How does genuine faith respond to those in need?

# JOURNAL

Do the questions or scripture reading from today stir your spirit or emotions in any way?

Is there an area in your life or in your faith that needs a deeper look?

## Study Questions

**Read James 2:17-18**

1.  How is faith without works described?

2.  Can genuine faith be separated from works?

3.  How is genuine faith proven or demonstrated in our lives?

--- PERSONAL ---

Does this knowledge encourage a change in your response to the needs of others?

What are some ways you can reach out to others to

share your faith, compassion, resources?

Use the Journal section to express your thoughts.

# JOURNAL

Do the questions or scripture reading from today stir your spirit or emotions in any way?

Is there an area in your life or in your faith that needs a deeper look?

## Study Questions

**Read Ephesians 2:8-9**

1.  How do we receive salvation?

2.  Name the gift and the giver of the gift.

3.  Is there anything we can do (works) in order to be saved?

4.  What is specifically excluded from our receiving salvation? What is the purpose for this exclusion?

# JOURNAL

Do the questions or scripture reading from today stir your spirit or emotions in any way?
Is there an area in your life or in your faith that needs a deeper look?

## Study Questions

**Read Ephesians 2:10**

1. For what purpose do we come to salvation?

2. Who has prepared these for us?

---

### PERSONAL

According to this verse, do you believe God has a purpose for your life?

What are your passions, gifts, and talents?
What do you enjoy more than anything?
Are these things aligned with scripture and with God's ways?
If so, perhaps His purpose and plan will manifest through these things.

In the Journal section, write a prayer asking God to show you what
He has planned for your life.

---

# JOURNAL

Do the questions or scripture reading from today stir your spirit or emotions in any way?
Is there an area in your life or in your faith that needs a deeper look?

## Study Questions

**Read 1 John 3:17**

1. As believers, what is our responsibility in meeting the needs of others?

2. How are we described when we refuse to meet needs?

3. Does this kind of attitude demonstrate genuine faith?

4. What is the relationship between God's love and works?

# JOURNAL

Do the questions or scripture reading from today stir your spirit or emotions in any way?

Is there an area in your life or in your faith that needs a deeper look?

## *Study Questions*

**Read Titus 3:8**

1. What is the charge given to believers?

2. Why are we given this instruction?

3. How often are we to affirm this truth?

# JOURNAL

Do the questions or scripture reading from today stir your spirit or emotions in any way?

Is there an area in your life or in your faith that needs a deeper look?

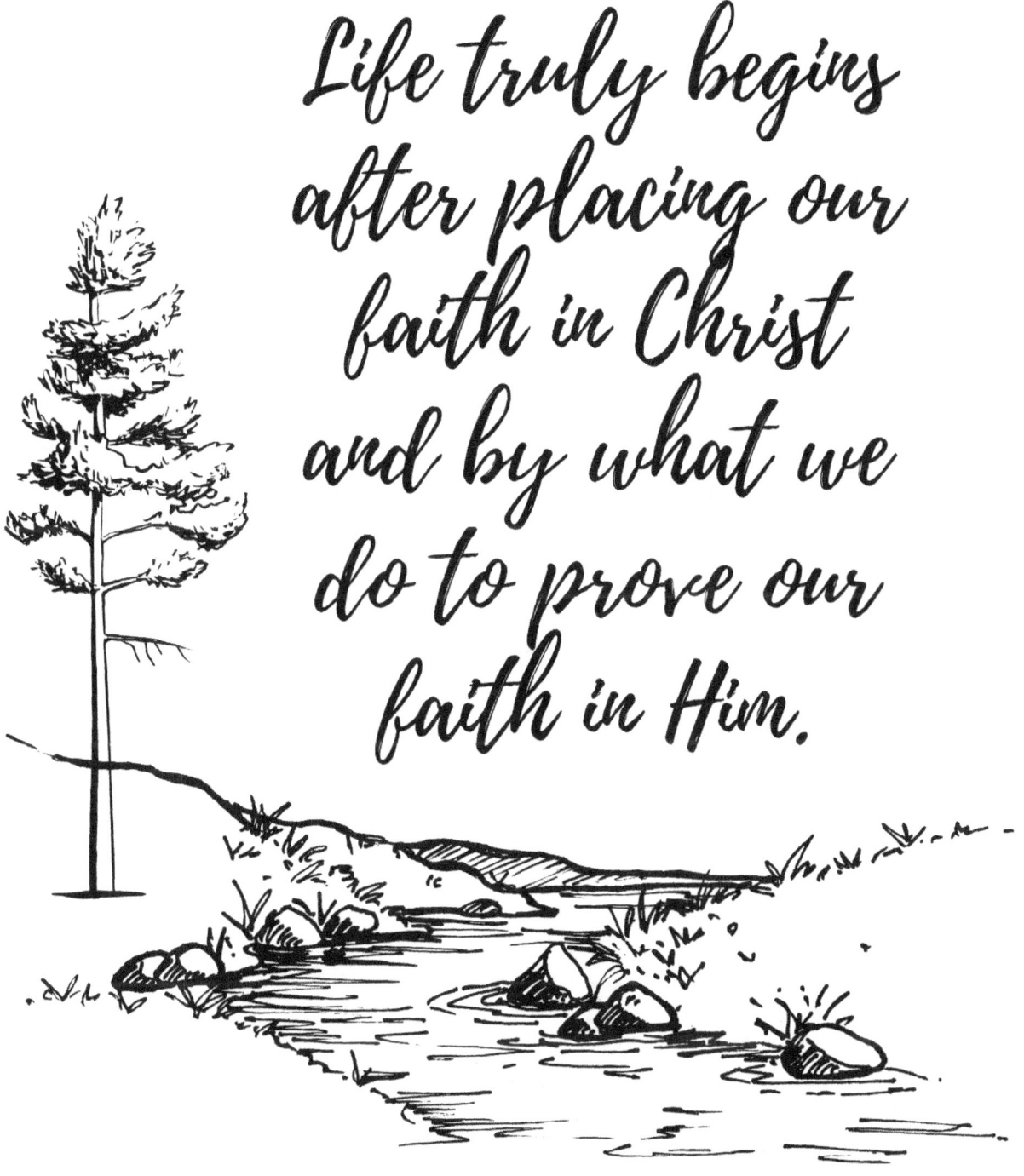

Life truly begins after placing our faith in Christ and by what we do to prove our faith in Him.

# 9

# Life and Death

*"You believe that there is one God. You do well. Even the demons believe—and tremble! But do you want to know, O foolish man, that faith without works is dead? Was not Abraham our father justified by works when he offered Isaac his son on the altar? Do you see that faith was working together with his works, and by works faith was made perfect? And the Scripture was fulfilled which says, 'Abraham believed God, and it was accounted to him for righteousness.' And he was called friend of God. You see then that a man is justified by works, and not by faith only.*

*"Likewise, was not Rahab the harlot also justified by works when she received the messengers and sent them out another way?*

*"For as the body without the spirit is dead, so faith without works is dead also."*

James 2:19-26

This lesson is a continuation from the previous lesson. Both define the relationship between faith and works. Belief that there is a God is not the same as having a relationship with Him, initiated through faith. James 2:19 exemplifies belief versus faith. James tells us that even the demons believe in God and tremble. In Matthew 8:28-29, Jesus is confronted by two demon possessed men. The demons themselves spoke to Jesus calling Him by name and then expressed fear and trembling when they asked Him if He was there to torment them "before time." Even demons believe there is One True God. They make mental ascent to Him. They acknowledge Jesus as the Son of God – Christ. The works of these demons who make mental ascent only to God are characterized by lies, deceit, devastation, destruction, and death. These works prove, while they may believe He exists, they do not have faith in God.

James goes on to say that genuine faith in God without works is not alive. We cannot work our way into faith, but if we have genuine faith, it will be proven by what we do. Genuine faith produces works characterized by truth and the fruit of the Holy Spirit. These works make a difference for good in the lives of others and give evidence of a living and vibrant faith in God. With this truth in mind, we are compelled to ask ourselves if we are continually seeking God and what He would have us do to further His kingdom and His work.

When we follow our own plans and fail to ask God for His plan, we create huge messes and then expect God to fix them. Isaac was not Abraham's only son! In Sarah's attempt to "help" God accomplish His purpose, instead of waiting for His perfect plan and timing, she created a mess, and we are still suffering the consequences of her failure to wait on God. The birth of Ishmael through Sarah's handmaid is the result of Sarah's impatience. Ishmael is the father of the Arab nations and the Muslim religion. Until Christ comes, there will always be division between the descendants of Isaac and Ishmael.

Abraham was a man of faith. He believed in God, and he believed God. He walked by faith and not by sight. His faith was accounted to him as righteousness and his faith justified him before God. His obedience proved his faith before men. Our obedience declares the reality of God without our saying a word. Abraham acted immediately according to God's instructions. He didn't have to think about it or form a committee; he just obeyed.

There are many examples of faith proven by works in the Bible, but James uses the examples of Abraham and Rahab.

*Abraham*

In Genesis 15, God made a promise to Abram for an heir, and not just one heir, but innumerable descendants. After God made His promise, Abraham believed God and it was accounted to him as righteousness. Notice that Abraham didn't "do" anything, he simply placed his faith in God and received the promise. It was his faith in God that declared him righteous.

When God told Abraham to take his son Isaac and offer him as a burnt offering, he had an opportunity to exercise faith in God and prove his faith by doing what God said. Abraham obeyed. When he reached the place where he and Isaac would have to leave their young men behind, Abraham, by faith, told them to stay with the donkey and both he AND Isaac would return. Abraham prepared everything for the sacrifice, but when he raised his knife to slay Isaac, the Angel of the Lord stopped him, and a ram was provided for the sacrifice. Abraham could not see how God would provide but he believed God, and his works then declared his faith. Abraham's innumerable descendants are still being counted as more and more come to faith in Jesus Christ.

*Rahab*

In Joshua 2, we learn about Rahab, a pagan and a prostitute, in the land of Jericho. She is named in the lineage of Jesus. When the spies came to her as they were viewing the land at Joshua's request, she told them she had heard of Jehovah and all He had done for the Israelites. She made a faith declaration when she said, "The Lord your God, He is God in heaven above and on earth beneath." She heard the testimonies of God and believed in her heart, then confessed with her mouth. It was her belief in God that motivated her to assist the spies.

I don't believe Rahab's lifestyle or the fact that she lied and deceived in order to help the spies were honoring to God. She was not perfect nor mature in her faith, but she was willing and available. Her belief in the One True God was demonstrated by her actions (works) and thus changed her destiny and that of her family. Rahab's actions proved her faith in God.

Just as the body without the spirit is dead, faith without works is dead. The body represents our faith, and the spirit represents our obedience through service. Our works prove and give life to our faith. Without works our faith is not purposeful. We are not defined by our lives or choices prior to coming to Christ in faith. Life truly begins after placing our faith in Christ and by what we do (works) to prove our faith in Him.

## ADDITIONAL SCRIPTURE

Genesis 22:1-14

Joshua 2:1-24

Matthew 8:28-29

Romans 10:10, 17

Titus 3:8

## PRAYER

Father, through Your Word, help me come to a
clear understanding of faith and works.
Show me how to appropriate genuine faith
through the service I do for You in Your Kingdom.
Give me rest from striving to "do" for You
and help me realize that simple faith is what pleases You.
Amen.

# Study Questions

**Read James 2:19**

1. Do the demons believe there is one God?

**Read Matthew 8:28**

2. Who confronted Jesus?

3. How are they described?

4. What problem did their presence create?

# JOURNAL

Do the questions or scripture reading from today stir your spirit or emotions in any way?

Is there an area in your life or in your faith that needs a deeper look?

## Study Questions

**Read Matthew 8:29**

1. What did the demons cry out?

2. Does this prove they have knowledge of Jesus and God?

3. What were they afraid Jesus would do?

4. Is this evidence of demons trembling?

---

### CHALLENGE

**Read Revelation 20.**

What do you think is meant by "before the time?" Explain your answer in the Journal section.

---

# JOURNAL

Do the questions or scripture reading from today stir your spirit or emotions in any way?

Is there an area in your life or in your faith that needs a deeper look?

## Study Questions

**Read James 2:20**

1. How does James address his readers?

2. How does he describe the relationship between faith and works?

**Read Titus 3:8**

3. What instruction does Titus give to believers?

4. What does he say is the effect of these?

# JOURNAL

Do the questions or scripture reading from today stir your spirit or emotions in any way?

Is there an area in your life or in your faith that needs a deeper look?

**Read James 2:21-23**

1. What is Abraham called?

2. **Read Genesis 22:1-14** to explain why he is called this.

3. Define justified.

4. By what does James 2:21 say Abraham was justified? Do you think this implies that works gain us favor with God?

---

**CHALLENGE**

**Read Genesis 22:5.**

How does this verse prove that Abraham
was a man of faith? Explain your
answer in the Journal section.

---

# JOURNAL

Do the questions or scripture reading from today stir your spirit or emotions in any way?

Is there an area in your life or in your faith that needs a deeper look?

## Study Questions

**Read James 2:22-24**

1.  Describe the inseparable union between faith and works.

2.  Which one must come first? Can we work our way into faith?

**Read Genesis 15:6**

3.  Is it possible to have faith and not have works? What is the proof of genuine faith? What was accounted to Abraham as righteousness?

4.  How is the relationship between God and Abraham described?

# JOURNAL

Do the questions or scripture reading from today stir your spirit or emotions in any way?
Is there an area in your life or in your faith that needs a deeper look?

## DAY 6
### Study Questions

**Read James 2:25-26**

1. What was Rahab's profession?


**Read Joshua 2:1-24**

2. Write a summary of how Rahab came to faith in God.



3. In James 2:26, what do works do for faith?


---

**PERSONAL**

Looking at Rahab's outward appearance (pagan, harlot),
would you have seen value in her or her usefulness to God?

Are you surprised to see her listed in the family lineage of Jesus?
Does this fact increase hope within you?

---

**CHALLENGE**

**Read Romans 10:10, 17**

Correlate Rahab's experience with these scriptures.
What does this teach us about judging others based on
their past? Record your thoughts in the Journal section.

# JOURNAL

Do the questions or scripture reading from today stir your spirit or emotions in any way?

Is there an area in your life or in your faith that needs a deeper look?

ULTIMATELY, GOD WILL BE REVEALED IN US THROUGH THE

*disciplined*

COURSE OF OUR WORDS.

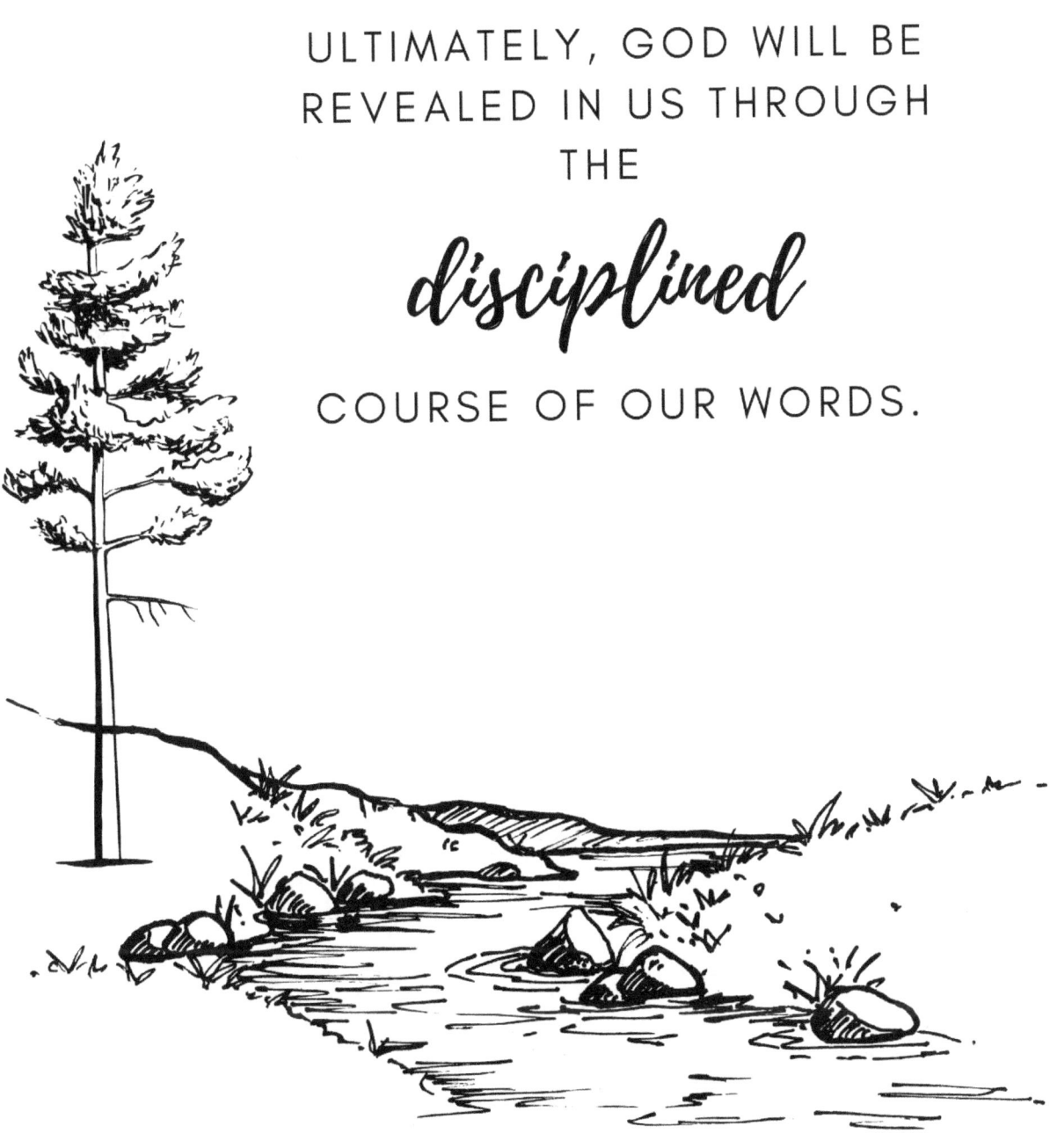

# The Power of the Tongue

*"My brethren, let not many of you become teachers, knowing that we shall receive a stricter judgment. For we all stumble in many things. If anyone does not stumble in word, he is a perfect man, able also to bridle the whole body. Indeed, we put bits in horses' mouths that they may obey us, and we turn their whole body. Look also at ships: although they are so large and are driven by fierce winds, they are turned by a very small rudder wherever the pilot desires. Even so the tongue is a little member and boasts great things.*

*"See how great a forest a little fire kindles! And the tongue is a fire, a world of iniquity. The tongue is so set among our members that it defiles the whole body, and sets on fire the course of nature; and it is set on fire by hell. For every kind of beast and bird, of reptile and creature of the sea, is tamed and has been tamed by mankind. But no man can tame the tongue. It is an unruly evil, full of deadly poison. With it we bless our God and Father, and with it we curse men, who have been made in the similitude of God. Out of the same mouth proceed blessing and cursing. My brethren, these things ought not to be so. Does a spring send forth fresh water and bitter from the same opening? Can a fig tree, my brethren, bear olives, or a grapevine bear figs? Thus no spring yields both salt water and fresh."*

James 3:1-12

If anyone ever asks us if we are packin' (carrying a weapon), our answer should be a resounding YES! We carry with us, everywhere we go, the most powerful and lethal weapon on the planet – our tongue. With this one, single, tiny weapon we have the ability to:

Wound or heal
Bless or curse
Build up or tear down
Praise or blaspheme

Comfort or cause anxiety

Bring unity and peace or strife and division

Give truth or lie

Change the entire course of a nation and history

Encourage or discourage

Empower or handicap

Breathe life or destroy life

Speak hope or remove all hope

Assassinate or murder the character of another

In the Bible, the tongue is compared to a bit in a horse's mouth, a rudder on a big ship, and a destructive fire. A bit needs a horseman, a rudder needs a ship's captain, and fires need firemen. Our tongue, though small, is powerful and needs directing as well. Words need something specifically designed to direct their course; this is the job of the Holy Spirit.

The Holy Spirit has been given to us and is perfectly capable of controlling our tongue. He is also able to quench the fire before it has a chance to cause destruction. We have the Holy Spirit, but the question is how much of us does He have? We need to allow Him to speak through us and direct us as He desires. Ultimately, He will be revealed in us through the disciplined course of our words. Whatever rolls off our tongue reveals what truly fills our heart.

Furthermore, I believe our words are eternal. If we had proper technology, each sound wave, every word spoken, could be captured and reproduced. Matthew 12:36-37 tells us that God has always had the technology to reveal the things we have spoken. This is a scary thought for sure; no wonder the Word tells us to study or learn to be quiet. The Word also teaches that we should speak ONLY those things which edify and lend grace to those who are hearing our words.

We will all stumble in our words at some point, but we should always be mindful of the need to control rather than be controlled by our tongue. Though it seems an impossibility, we should always work on taming our tongues. If we demonstrate self-control concerning our speech, then having self-control in other areas of our lives should be a piece of cake. The Word tells us whatever fills our hearts comes out of our mouths. To effectively control the tongue, we will have to work on our hearts. When we place our faith in Jesus Christ, we receive a new heart. In order to promote a healthy heart, we must remain in God's Word. Studying and applying God's Word protects us from heart disease.

Let's ask the Lord to set a watch over our mouths and keep the door of our lips. Let's challenge ourselves to speak words of life. These words are full of encouragement, edification, blessing, and affirmation.

# ADDITIONAL SCRIPTURE

Psalm 141:3

Matthew 12:34-37

Matthew 15:18-19

Ephesians 4:29

## PRAYER

Father, teach me to guard my heart and mind in Christ Jesus, through Your Word.

Let my heart be filled with a desire to glorify You and bless others.

Amen.

## Study Questions

**Read James 3:1-6**

1.  What is the warning for those who desire to become teachers? Who stumbles in many things?

2.  What is the key to self-control?

3.  List the things James compares with the tongue.

4.  Describe the impact of each.

# JOURNAL

Do the questions or scripture reading from today stir your spirit or emotions in any way?
Is there an area in your life or in your faith that needs a deeper look?

# Study Questions

**Read James 3:7-12**

1. What has man been able to tame?

2. What is the one thing man has not been able to conquer or tame?

3. Name and further describe the two ways in which we use our tongue.

4. Does this seem contrary to the purpose God intended for its use? Give the analogies used to describe this contradiction.

# JOURNAL

Do the questions or scripture reading from today stir your spirit or emotions in any way?

Is there an area in your life or in your faith that needs a deeper look?

## Study Questions

**Read Matthew 15:18-19**

1. Where do our words originate?

2. How do our words impact us?

3. List other things which originate in our hearts.

---

### PERSONAL

As you examine your heart, are there things the Holy Spirit needs to change?
Are there things you desire to change but do not have the willpower
or self-control to manage on your own? Use the Journal section to
invite the Holy Spirit into these areas of your life, asking Him to give
you strength, endurance, and grace to overcome these things.

---

# JOURNAL

Do the questions or scripture reading from today stir your spirit or emotions in any way?

Is there an area in your life or in your faith that needs a deeper look?

# Study Questions

**Read Matthew 12:34-37**

1. Find the impossibility in these verses.

2. What are the two natural outcomes depending on the condition of the heart.

3. Do our words matter?

4. What are the ways in which our words impact our lives?

# JOURNAL

Do the questions or scripture reading from today stir your spirit or emotions in any way?

Is there an area in your life or in your faith that needs a deeper look?

# Study Questions

**Read Ephesians 4:29**

1. What are we to keep from coming out of our mouths?

2. What is meant when it says "unwholesome" talk?

3. For what purpose are we to use our mouths?

4. When we build others up with our words, what do we impart to them?

# JOURNAL

Do the questions or scripture reading from today stir your spirit or emotions in any way?

Is there an area in your life or in your faith that needs a deeper look?

## — DAY 6 —
## *Study Questions*

**Read Psalm 141:3**

1.   Who is able to tame our tongue?

2.   What two things should we ask for in order to accomplish this?

**Read Psalm 19:14**

3.   Rewrite this verse and insert your name.

---

### CHALLENGE

Find verses in scripture that teach how to guard
and fill your heart. Whatever fills your heart
will be demonstrated in your words and actions.
Use the verses below to get started, then see
how many more you can find. For more space,
use the Journal section to record your answers.

Psalm 66:18       Matthew 22:37a
Psalm 119:7-8a     1 Peter 3:15a
Psalm 119:9       Ephesians 6:6
Proverbs 4:23

---

# JOURNAL

Do the questions or scripture reading from today stir your spirit or emotions in any way?

Is there an area in your life or in your faith that needs a deeper look?

The fruit of righteousness is reflected in our lives and will never be produced from soil rich in harshness, hatefulness, or a quarrelsome spirit.

# Two Kinds of Wisdom

*"Who is wise and understanding among you? Let him show by good conduct that his works are done in the meekness of wisdom. But if you have bitter envy and self-seeking in your hearts, do not boast and lie against the truth. This wisdom does not descend from above, but is earthly, sensual, demonic. For where envy and self-seeking exist, confusion and every evil thing are there. But the wisdom that is from above is first pure, then peaceable, gentle, willing to yield, full of mercy and good fruits, without partiality and without hypocrisy. Now the fruit of righteousness is sown in peace by those who make peace."*

James 3:13-18

Understanding comes through the application of knowledge. Wisdom is the combining of knowledge plus understanding. Wisdom is not something stored in our heads but is reflected in our behavior and lifestyle. Wisdom is not some kind of philosophy; it is a critical skill used in problem solving: social, economic, and spiritual. It is practical for everything and every day in our lives. The source or beginning of wisdom is the fear (reverential awe) of the Lord. There are two kinds of wisdom: earthly and heavenly.

| Earthly Wisdom | Heavenly Wisdom |
|---|---|
| Sensual, demonic | Pure, peaceable, gentle |
| Bitter envy | Willing to yield |
| Self-seeking | Full of mercy and good fruits |
| Confusion and every evil work | Without partiality |
| Does damage to others | Without hypocrisy |
| Looks out for self (number one) | Accomplishes the work of God |
| | Blesses others |
| | Looks out for others |

The fruit of wisdom is righteousness. The fruit of righteousness is reflected in the lives we live and the righteous deeds done. Peace is the fertile soil in which the fruit of righteousness grows and is sown only by those who make peace. We must have peace with God and peace with others. Lasting peace comes from peace with God, through relationship with Him. The fruit of righteousness will never be produced from soil rich in harshness, hatefulness, or a quarrelsome spirit.

Jesus said,
*"Peace I leave with you, My peace I give to you."*
John 14:27

We have everything we need!

## ADDITIONAL SCRIPTURE

Job 28:12, 28
John 14:27

### PRAYER

Father, give me the wisdom I need to use my words in ways
that touch hearts and change lives.
Use me to make a difference for good in this world until Christ comes again.
Amen.

## Study Questions

**Read James 3:13**

1. How is wisdom demonstrated in our lives?

2. Describe the way in which our works should be done.

3. Define meekness.

4. What is meant by "the meekness of wisdom"?

# JOURNAL

Do the questions or scripture reading from today stir your spirit or emotions in any way?
Is there an area in your life or in your faith that needs a deeper look?

# Study Questions

**Read James 3:14-16**

1. Define bitter envy. Define self-seeking.

2. What is the result of harboring these things in our hearts?

3. List the words used to describe earthly wisdom.

4. What is the result of envy and self-seeking in our lives?

# JOURNAL

Do the questions or scripture reading from today stir your spirit or emotions in any way?

Is there an area in your life or in your faith that needs a deeper look?

# Study Questions

**Read James 3:17-18**

1.  List words used to describe God's wisdom.



2.  Define partiality. Define hypocrisy. Explain why partiality and hypocrisy are not part of God's wisdom.



3.  Describe the manner in which the fruit of righteousness is sown. Who is able to sow in this manner?



4.  Define peace. Define peacemaker.

# JOURNAL

Do the questions or scripture reading from today stir your spirit or emotions in any way?
Is there an area in your life or in your faith that needs a deeper look?

## Study Questions

**Read Job 28:12**

1. For what two things should we search?

**Read Job 28:28**

2. Where can these two things be found?

3. Define wisdom. Define understanding.

# JOURNAL

Do the questions or scripture reading from today stir your spirit or emotions in any way?

Is there an area in your life or in your faith that needs a deeper look?

# Study Questions

**Read John 14:27**

1.  From whom does peace come?

2.  Have we as believers been given this gift of peace?

3.  Describe the type of peace the world offers.

4.  What are we NOT to allow into our hearts and lives?

# JOURNAL

Do the questions or scripture reading from today stir your spirit or emotions in any way?

Is there an area in your life or in your faith that needs a deeper look?

## Study Questions

**Read 2 Timothy 1:7**

*Fear is an enemy to our faith and our peace.*

1.  List your fears in the first column below.
    In the second column, list attributes of God's peace to counter these fears.

| My Fears | God's Peace |
| --- | --- |
| Example: Worry about finances | Example: God is my provider |
|  |  |
|  |  |
|  |  |
|  |  |
|  |  |
|  |  |
|  |  |

2.  Rewrite 2 Timothy 1:7 inserting your name.




3.  In the Journal section, write a prayer giving your fears to Jesus, asking Him to replace your fears with His peace.

# JOURNAL

Do the questions or scripture reading from today stir your spirit or emotions in any way?

Is there an area in your life or in your faith that needs a deeper look?

THE HOLY SPIRIT IS
CONSTANTLY

*drawing us back
to Himself,*

AWAY FROM THE
ENTICEMENTS OF
THE WORLD.

# Ongoing Battle

*"Where do wars and fights come from among you? Do they not come from your desires for pleasure that war in your members? You lust and do not have. You murder and covet and cannot obtain. You fight and war. Yet you do not have because you do not ask. You ask and do not receive, because you ask amiss, that you may spend it on your pleasures. Adulterers and adulteresses! Do you not know that friendship with the world is enmity with God? Whoever therefore wants to be a friend of the world makes himself an enemy of God. Or do you think that the Scripture says in vain, 'The Spirit who dwells in us yearns jealously'?"*

James 4:1-5

Jesus spoke these words, lifted His eyes to heaven, and said,

*"I do not pray that You should take them out of the world, but that You should keep them from the evil one. They are not of the world, just as I am not of the world. Sanctify them by Your truth. Your word is truth."*

John 17:15-17

In today's scripture, we read about a matter that seems to be every believer's battle. Basically, the church was acting like the world. In His high priestly prayer from John 17, Jesus asked the Father to enable believers to maintain a clear demarcation between the world (unbelievers) and believers. The world system is in direct opposition to God and His ways. Jesus did not ask God to remove believers from this world and all that is in it. He asked the Father to keep the world out of us.

Jesus gives us a foolproof method for maintaining Christianity while living in the world:

Sanctify them (set them apart) by Your truth.
Then He clearly identifies the source of all truth – His Word.

Knowing and applying God's Word is our only hope for overcoming the hypnotic effects of the world and all it has to offer. We are to distinguish ourselves in every way from those who choose to live according to the world.

There is no mincing words or soft pedaling truth. James goes straight to the point in revealing the true reasons for the relational issues in the church.

*"But I see another law in my members, warring against the law of my mind, and bringing me into captivity to the law of sin which is in my members."*

Romans 7:23

There is a constant war raging inside every believer. This war stems from the two natures residing in us and they are contrary to one another. Let's compare it with a fight between a black dog and a white dog.

Black dog = flesh nature
White dog = spiritual nature

Which one are we feeding the most? The one we nurture and nourish is the one that will prevail.

In James 4:2, we see where internal war meets outlet. What has not been kept in check while raging on the inside will pour forth and manifest itself in deadly and destructive ways. Lust includes so much more than sexual desire or the desire for material possessions. It also includes a desire for power, position, prestige, and status.

James further explains that friendship with the world makes us an enemy of God. The term friend used here is more than just a casual acquaintance. It is affection for the world, it's ways and all that is in it. The Bible says we can't serve two masters. We will love the one and hate the other. To seek the things of this world places us in direct opposition to God.

The Lord God is ONE – He is a jealous God. He insists on preeminence in our lives. Just as a wife becomes jealous when she senses an intruder in relationship with her husband, so God is the same. It is love for our spouse that invokes that jealousy. It's a protective measure which is a healthy kind of jealousy. The Holy Spirit's presence in our lives is God Himself. He is constantly drawing us back to Himself away from the enticements of the world.

Let's ask God to align our desires with His will and then seek Him to fulfill those desires. Peace will reign within us, around us, and with God as well. Let us seek to do the will of God and He will keep the world out of us.

In chapter 4, James examines the origin of relational problems among believers.

The problem begins in the heart of an individual when strong desires for pleasure are not met.

The problem with others occurs when we look to them instead of looking to the Lord to fulfill our desires.

James says we not only ask God to supply, but we ask for the wrong reasons. We reach, grab, and try to take from others in order to get what we want. This is a form of spiritual idolatry because we trust in ourselves and others to supply what only God can supply. He not only supplies the desires within us, which align with His will for our lives, but He alone possesses the resources to provide for those desires.

In verse 4, James uses harsh words to describe us when we seek provision from any source other than God. When we do this, he says we are adulterers and adulteresses.

Adultery is being unfaithful to your spouse, thus breaking covenant. Jewish believers understood covenant relationship with God. God used a physical marriage analogy to describe the same covenant relationship in the spiritual realm. Believers are called the Bride of Christ. When we choose Jesus, we enter a covenant relationship with God. When we choose to pursue and indulge in the ways of the world, we commit spiritual adultery. All these passions drive us to fulfill ourselves no matter who we have to step on in order to obtain our desire.

The Bible is full of accounts concerning these. David's lust for Bathsheba began with a lust of the eyes. David "saw" her, then progressed to finding a way to meet with her, and his sin, once conceived, gave birth to adultery, murder, and the death of the child conceived in sin.

Worldly passions are both selfish and self-centered, as well as self-fulfilling. In other words, it's "all about me!" Yet it seems no matter how much we try to grab, we always find ourselves unsatisfied. It is in giving to and serving others where we find fulfillment and satisfaction. This is God's law of reciprocity at work.

In giving, we receive.
We receive in order to give.

Give of your money, time, gifts, and talents.
You will receive lasting satisfaction and fulfillment.

# ADDITIONAL SCRIPTURE

John 17:15-18

Romans 7:23

2 Corinthians 6:14-18

Ephesians 2:1-5

1 John 2:15-17

## PRAYER

Father, help me remember that I have to be IN this
world, but I am not OF this world.
The war has already been won, through the shed blood of Jesus Christ,
even though I have ongoing battles to fight.
Strengthen me through Your Word and remind me
daily to put on the full armor of God.

Amen.

## Study Questions

**Read John 17:15-18**

1. What is Jesus' desire for believers?

2. What does Jesus say about our citizenship?

3. What is the method for setting believers apart from the world?

4. Where is our mission field?

# JOURNAL

Do the questions or scripture reading from today stir your spirit or emotions in any way?
Is there an area in your life or in your faith that needs a deeper look?

# Study Questions

**Read Ephesians 2:1-5**

1. How is our life characterized prior to our salvation experience?

2. Under whose authority do unbelievers operate?

3. Who has been impacted by this ruler?

4. In what ways are the effects of this ruler manifested in people?

# JOURNAL

Do the questions or scripture reading from today stir your spirit or emotions in any way?

Is there an area in your life or in your faith that needs a deeper look?

*Study Questions*

**Read 2 Corinthians 6:14-18**

1.  What is the reasoning behind not being unequally yoked with unbelievers? Identify the two contrasts.

2.  How are believers described? As such, with what are we not to enter into agreement? Identify the relationship which makes us unique.

3.  What are our marching orders as believers?

4.  Describe our intimate relationship with the Lord Almighty.

# JOURNAL

Do the questions or scripture reading from today stir your spirit or emotions in any way?
Is there an area in your life or in your faith that needs a deeper look?

## *Study Questions*

**Read James 4:1-5**

1. What is the origin of wars and fights among believers? Name the four ways mentioned in which people try to fulfill their lusts.

2. What is listed as the reason our petitions are not granted.

3. What does James call believers who have left God, their first love? What harsh term is used to describe believers who want to be friends with the world?

4. God's Spirit dwells in us. How does His Spirit respond when we behave as spiritual adulterers?

---

### CHALLENGE

There are other reasons for unanswered prayer. For a deeper dive into the scriptures, see if you can identify some of those reasons, using

Psalm 66:18
Proverbs 28:9
Luke 18:11-14

List these reasons in the Journal section. Then see if you can find more scriptures to help identify other reasons.

---

# JOURNAL

Do the questions or scripture reading from today stir your spirit or emotions in any way?
Is there an area in your life or in your faith that needs a deeper look?

## Study Questions

**Read Romans 7:1-25**

*All believers experience the constant inner struggle.*
*Paul was no exception.*

1. Describe Paul's struggle.

2. What are the two natures at work in a believer?

3. What can believers do to ensure that our new nature wins the internal battle?

---
### PERSONAL

Can you identify with Paul's struggle? If so, in what way?

---

# JOURNAL

Do the questions or scripture reading from today stir your spirit or emotions in any way?

Is there an area in your life or in your faith that needs a deeper look?

# Study Questions

**Read 1 John 2:15-17**

1. Prior to your salvation experience, describe how your life reflected the world's standards.

2. Describe the changes in your life after receiving Christ.

3. List the methods you can use in maintaining your Christian walk.

4. What is passing away? Who will live forever?

# JOURNAL

Do the questions or scripture reading from today stir your spirit or emotions in any way?

Is there an area in your life or in your faith that needs a deeper look?

GOD RESISTS OR SETS
HIMSELF AGAINST THOSE
WHO ARE PROUD, BUT

*He pours out grace to those who are humble.*

# Grace for the Win!

*"But He gives more grace. Therefore He says:*
*'God resists the proud,*
*But gives grace to the humble'*

*"Therefore submit to God. Resist the devil and he will flee from you. Draw near to God and*
*He will draw near to you. Cleanse your hands, you sinners; and purify your hearts, you*
*double-minded. Lament and mourn and weep! Let your laughter be turned to mourning and*
*your joy to gloom. Humble yourselves in the sight of the Lord, and He will lift you up."*

James 4:6-10

God's grace enables us to have victory over the draw of worldly desire or pleasure which causes us to turn away from God. God has manifold grace for manifold temptation. Manifold means many or varied. He has grace to match anything that comes our way, and He is willing to give more grace.

The scriptures reveal that grace has a requirement – humility. God resists or sets Himself against, in order to defeat, those who are proud, but He gives (pours out) grace to those who are humble. Those who are proud are arrogant and think they are above others. The key to receiving God's grace is humility. We need to recognize, acknowledge, and confess our inability to overcome. To be humble is to depend on God and His ability to accomplish in us what is needed to stay the course and remain focused.

James gives us the formula for success:

**Submit to God.**

Submit means to surrender; to yield one's power to another. When we submit to God, we humble ourselves and open the door through which grace can flow.

**Resist.**

Resist literally means to stand against; to withstand; to strive against; to endeavor to counteract, defeat, or frustrate.

**Draw near to God.**

God is always waiting for us to tuck under His protective wing.

We are not the ones who should run. We are to stand under the authority of God Almighty. When children are afraid, they run to their parents for protection.

The logical question is, how do we draw near to God? We do so by practicing the following:

We spend time reading and meditating on His Word.

We communicate with God through prayer. We pour out our heart to Him, taking time to listen to what He wants to say. Prayer is a two-way communication. Prayer is not just our opportunity to bring a laundry list of petitions to Him. Pray and listen.

As we draw near to Him, He promises to draw near to us and, in the process, He becomes magnified. Every time we drive to the mountains, I anticipate their majesty from far away. The further away we are, the smaller the mountains appear. The closer we get to the mountains, the more they are magnified (become larger). They continue to get larger as we draw closer until all we see is their majesty. Like those mountains, the closer we draw to God the more we behold His majesty!

Repent and confess sin. Be cleansed. He is faithful to cleanse us from ALL unrighteousness.

Our hearts must be broken over our sin. We must grieve over sin. Weeping over our sin is an outward manifestation of inward brokenness.

The more we know God, the more we understand that He is holy and just. As we come to this understanding, we realize our helplessness and hopelessness. We are totally depraved apart from God. When we bow to Him (humble ourselves). He does not squash us, He exalts us. What a great God.

# ADDITIONAL SCRIPTURE

Isaiah 1:16-18

Ephesians 4:25-29

1 John 1:9

## PRAYER

Father, give me the peace I need to surrender to You

so I can resist the devil and his schemes that work to undermine my faith.

As I draw near to You, draw near to me, and allow me to sense Your presence.

In Your presence is where I find peace, strength, and joy everlasting!

Amen.

## Study Questions

**Read James 4:6**

1. Is God's grace limited?

2. Whom does God resist?

3. Define resist.

4. To whom does God give grace? Define humble.

# JOURNAL

Do the questions or scripture reading from today stir your spirit or emotions in any way?

Is there an area in your life or in your faith that needs a deeper look?

## Study Questions

**Read James 4:7-10**

1. List ways in which we submit to God. What is the result of resisting the devil?

2. What is the benefit of drawing near to God? List the actions we need to take in order to draw near to God.

3. Define double-minded.

4. What should be our attitude toward sin? What is God's response as we humble ourselves in His sight?

# JOURNAL

Do the questions or scripture reading from today stir your spirit or emotions in any way?

Is there an area in your life or in your faith that needs a deeper look?

# Study Questions

**Read Ephesians 4:23-24**

1.  What is our first step after salvation in resisting the devil?

2.  Describe the second step in resisting the devil.

3.  Describe the qualities of the "new man."

# JOURNAL

Do the questions or scripture reading from today stir your spirit or emotions in any way?

Is there an area in your life or in your faith that needs a deeper look?

## DAY 4
### Study Questions

**Read Ephesians 4:25-29**

1. Fill in the chart below. On one side, list the ways Satan manifests himself in our lives. On the other side, list the qualities of the Spirit-led life which counteract and replace the negative characteristics.

| Read Ephesians 4:25-29 | |
| --- | --- |
| **Ways Satan Manifests in our Lives** | **Qualities of the Spirit-led Life** |
|  |  |
|  |  |
|  |  |
|  |  |
|  |  |

2. Is it alright to be angry?

3. What is specifically named as opening a door of opportunity for the devil?

4. In your opinion, how can you guard against opening the door for the devil?

# JOURNAL

Do the questions or scripture reading from today stir your spirit or emotions in any way?

Is there an area in your life or in your faith that needs a deeper look?

## *Study Questions*

**Read 1 John 1:9**

1.  What are we encouraged to do?

2.  If we do our part, what is God faithful to do?

3.  Does God leave anything for us to clean up?

4.  Is there anything/any area in your life that needs to be brought before God for cleansing and healing? Use the Journal section to write a prayer to God asking for His cleansing, healing, and guidance.

# JOURNAL

Do the questions or scripture reading from today stir your spirit or emotions in any way?

Is there an area in your life or in your faith that needs a deeper look?

# Study Questions

**Read Isaiah 1:16-18**

1.  After we apply the spiritual bar of soap, what does God say we must do?

2.  God does not remove anything damaging from our lives without replacing it with something constructive. What commands does He give to us?

3.  What invitation is extended to believers?

4.  How is sin described prior to repentance? How is sin described after our salvation experience?

# JOURNAL

Do the questions or scripture reading from today stir your spirit or emotions in any way?

Is there an area in your life or in your faith that needs a deeper look?

Our speech
reveals what is
in our hearts.

# Judging Others

*"Do not speak evil of one another, brethren. He who speaks evil of a brother and judges his brother, speaks evil of the law and judges the law. But if you judge the law, you are not a doer of the law but a judge. There is one Lawgiver, who is able to save and to destroy. Who are you to judge another?"*

James 4:11-12

It is unusual for a Bible study to focus an entire lesson on just two verses, but this topic is worthy of deeper study. There is another area of our lives in which we need grace for the win - our speech. With our mouths we bless God and curse others; this is an ongoing battle all believers must fight.

Evil speaking or slander refers to mindless, careless, critical, derogatory, untrue speech directed against others. The one place we should be free from this kind of talk is in our churches, among the family of God – believers. We can expect this kind of cruelty from unbelievers, but it should never characterize Christians. Though it is sad to say, I have both witnessed and experienced more evil speaking and judgmental attitudes from those in the church as opposed to those outside the church.

The type of speech addressed in this lesson is not about assessing or evaluating for the purpose of correction, it is more about judging and condemning another. Our speech reveals what is in our hearts. When we speak evil of others, in effect, we are judging them. So how does this relate to the law? Jesus said the law could be summed up in two statements:

*"Love the Lord your God with all your heart, mind soul and strength,*
*and love your neighbor as yourself."*

When we speak evil of others, we decide the law does not apply to us and, therefore, make ourselves above the law, as judge, jury, and executioner of others. Only God sits on the "judicial bench." No one else is qualified to judge others.

In the book of Matthew, Jesus warns against judging others. He confirms that we have no right to judge others and He says we invite the same judgement on ourselves.

We have an antidote for evil speaking:
We are to encourage one another every chance we get and
build each other up.

In Ephesians, Paul instructs believers, when we talk, we are not to say harmful things. Rather, we are to say what people need – words that help them grow, develop character, and become stronger.
In his devotional, *Grace for the Moment*, author Max Lucado says,

"You have the ability with your words to make a person stronger. Your words are to their soul what a vitamin is to their body. Do not withhold encouragement from the discouraged. Do not keep affirmation from the beaten down! Speak words that make people stronger. Believe in them as God has believed in you."[4]

This is truly wisdom from above. As we work through this study, let's ask God to reveal areas in which we need to grow in order to speak words of life to those around us.

## ADDITIONAL SCRIPTURE

Exodus 20:1-21
Matthew 7:1-5
Ephesians 4:29
1 Peter 2:1-3

## PRAYER

Father, help me use my words to encourage and build others up.
All around me, people are hurting and need to hear
a word, in season, to lift their weary soul.
Show me those in my path who need to hear life-giving words.
Keep me ever mindful of the fact that I am not to judge others.
Amen.

## Study Questions

**Read James 4:11-12**

1.  What changes can we make that would help to prevent speaking evil of and judging others?

---

—— PERSONAL ——

Have you ever judged someone?
On the Journal page, describe the circumstances for making that judgement.

Have you ever been guilty of speaking evil of another person?
On the Journal page, write a prayer asking God to help in this area.

---

# JOURNAL

Do the questions or scripture reading from today stir your spirit or emotions in any way?

Is there an area in your life or in your faith that needs a deeper look?

## Study Questions

**Read James 4:11**

1  List some ways in which we speak evil of others.

2.  What does the Word say about speaking evil of others?

3.  Who are our brethren (brothers/sisters)?

4.  When we speak evil of and judge our brother, of what are we also guilty?

# JOURNAL

Do the questions or scripture reading from today stir your spirit or emotions in any way?

Is there an area in your life or in your faith that needs a deeper look?

# Study Questions

**Read James 4:11**

1. What do we cease doing when we judge the law?

2. What then do we become?

**Read 1 Peter 2:1-3**

3. List characteristics we are to lay aside.

4. What action should we take to ensure our success with laying aside those characteristics?

# JOURNAL

Do the questions or scripture reading from today stir your spirit or emotions in any way?
Is there an area in your life or in your faith that needs a deeper look?

## Study Questions

**Read James 4:12**

1. How many lawgivers are there?

**Read Exodus 20:1**

2. Who is THE lawgiver? To whom was the law given?

3. For whom was the law given?

# JOURNAL

Do the questions or scripture reading from today stir your spirit or emotions in any way?

Is there an area in your life or in your faith that needs a deeper look?

## Study Questions

**Read Matthew 7:1-5**

1. List two things Jesus warns will happen if we judge others.

2. What does Jesus say we should do before we try to correct someone?

3. What does Jesus call those who judge others without first evaluating themselves?

4. Define hypocrite.

# JOURNAL

Do the questions or scripture reading from today stir your spirit or emotions in any way?

Is there an area in your life or in your faith that needs a deeper look?

# Study Questions

**Read Ephesians 4:29**

1. What should we prevent our mouths from doing? What should we allow in our speech?

2. Define edify.

3. What do we impart to those whom we edify?

4. In the journal section, make a list of words that edify.

---

**CHALLENGE**

Write a letter of encouragement to
someone using words that edify.

---

# JOURNAL

Do the questions or scripture reading from today stir your spirit or emotions in any way?

Is there an area in your life or in your faith that needs a deeper look?

MAKING PLANS WITHOUT
SEEKING GOD IS A
RIDICULOUS MINDSET.

*Only God knows what the future holds.*

# 15

# Depend on the Lord

*"Come now, you who say, 'Today or tomorrow we will go to such and such a city, spend a year there, buy and sell, and make a profit'; whereas you do not know what will happen tomorrow. For what is your life? It is even a vapor that appears for a little time and then vanishes away. Instead you ought to say, 'If the Lord wills, we shall live and do this or that.' But now you boast in your arrogance. All such boasting is evil.*

*"Therefore to him who knows to do good and does not do it, to him it is sin."*

James 4:13-17

A successful business begins with planning. The scripture above describes the elements of our plans:

| | |
|---|---|
| When? | Today or tomorrow |
| Where? | Such and such a city |
| How long? | A year |
| Itinerary? | Buy and sell |
| Net result or goal? | Make a profit |

Any good, solid plan would take these things into account. There is only one problem – there is no mention of God in this plan. It is not wrong to make plans; however, we get into trouble when we leave God out of our plans. We have a natural tendency to devise a plan and then expect God to rubber stamp and bless our plan.

The very first step in devising any successful plan is to seek God in prayer. We are to tell Him what is on our heart and then ask Him to give us wisdom in planning. Making plans without seeking God is a ridiculous mindset. Only God knows what the future holds. When put into perspective, our lives are no longer than the vapor of our breath on a cold day. Life is short. We are to make it count. We should always consult the Lord before making and carrying out our plans. We can ask God to show us His will and be willing to alter our plans as He leads.

Excluding God from our planning exhibits excessive pride in our ability to make our own path and demonstrates presumptuousness or overstepping our bounds. When we know God's mind on any issue yet don't do as He says, we have sinned. He desires to be central in every aspect of our lives and takes it very seriously when we exclude or dismiss Him. We are to make our plans but seek God FIRST.

## ADDITIONAL SCRIPTURE

Job 7:7

Psalm 19:13

1 John 1:9

## PRAYER

Father, give me guidance and direction as I make plans for each day of my life.

Help me remember to seek You first each day as my number one priority.

As I trust You, please bless me as I go through each day.

Let me be a blessing to others.

Amen.

## Study Questions

**Read James 4:13**

1. There is an obvious omission from this plan; what is it?

2. List the elements of a good plan.

3. What should be our first step in making a plan?

---

### PERSONAL

Have you ever devised a good, solid plan, only to see it fail?
How does today's lesson help you find the remedy for future planning?

---

# JOURNAL

Do the questions or scripture reading from today stir your spirit or emotions in any way?

Is there an area in your life or in your faith that needs a deeper look?

# Study Questions

**Read James 4:14**

1. Do we know what our future holds?

2. How is our life described?

**Read Job 7:7**

3. How does Job describe his own life?

4. In light of eternity, how long is our life?

# JOURNAL

Do the questions or scripture reading from today stir your spirit or emotions in any way?

Is there an area in your life or in your faith that needs a deeper look?

## Study Questions

**Read James 4:15**

1. What should be our first consideration in making plans?

2. Should God's will be sought for every area of our lives?

3. In the Journal section, write a prayer asking God to reveal His will for your life.

---

**CHALLENGE**

Can we know God's will?

**Read Romans 2:18** to support your
answer. Journal your thoughts.

---

# JOURNAL

Do the questions or scripture reading from today stir your spirit or emotions in any way?

Is there an area in your life or in your faith that needs a deeper look?

# Study Questions

**Read James 4:16**

1. Define boast. What does the Bible say about boasting?

2. List some synonyms for boast.

3. Define arrogance.

4. List some synonyms for arrogance.

# JOURNAL

Do the questions or scripture reading from today stir your spirit or emotions in any way?

Is there an area in your life or in your faith that needs a deeper look?

## Study Questions

**Read Psalm 19:13**

1. Define presumptuous.

2. What is the Psalmist asking God to do for him?

3. What are we guilty of when we deliberately disregard doing good?

4. Write 1 John 1:9 and insert your name.

# JOURNAL

Do the questions or scripture reading from today stir your spirit or emotions in any way?
Is there an area in your life or in your faith that needs a deeper look?

# Study Questions

## PERSONAL

List areas in your life where you need to trust the Lord.

Include things that make you fearful, anxious, and cause you worry.
Include insecurities, doubts, and questions.

# JOURNAL

Do the questions or scripture reading from today stir your spirit or emotions in any way?

Is there an area in your life or in your faith that needs a deeper look?

We must cultivate
and maintain a heart
of giving.

IN DOING SO, WE OPEN
THE DOOR TO GOD'S
ABUNDANT BLESSING IN
OUR LIVES.

# Faith and Riches

*"Come now, you rich, weep and howl for your miseries that are coming upon you! Your riches are corrupted, and your garments are moth-eaten. Your gold and silver are corroded, and their corrosion will be a witness against you and will eat your flesh like fire. You have heaped up treasure in the last days. Indeed the wages of the laborers who mowed your fields, which you kept back by fraud, cry out; and the cries of the reapers have reached the ears of the Lord of Sabaoth. You have lived on the earth in pleasure and luxury; you have fattened your hearts as in the day of slaughter. You have condemned, you have murdered the just; he does not resist you."*

James 5:1-6

If this scripture is read without context, it would appear to be an indictment against people who have wealth. However, this passage is not about possessions, but rather heart attitudes.

Those whose heart is set on acquiring wealth for the sake of greed will certainly exchange their comfort for misery when they stand before God's throne. However, if their heart is set on the Lord and He increases wealth for them, then their heart attitude will be one of giving, generosity, and looking for opportunities to bless others. This passage clearly teaches us that wealth -- material possessions -- are temporary, not eternal. This kind of treasure does not transfer to heaven.

In the gospel of Matthew, Jesus uses a litmus test for the heart attitude concerning wealth. Would we be able to pass the test? In the gospel of Luke, God says we are a fool if we store up treasures for ourselves but are not rich toward God. (See Matthew 19:16-22, Luke 12:15-21) There are many examples in scripture that clearly point to God's desire to bless us with material possessions and wealth, but our hearts must be fully devoted to Him.

Abraham was very rich; he had livestock, silver, and gold. When the children of Israel left Egypt, the Lord gave them favor with the Egyptians and they left Egypt with clothing, silver, and gold. After

Job repented and came to the Lord, he was restored double the amount of what he had even before the testing began. Keep in mind that he was wealthy before he went through the trials. The book of Proverbs is filled with wisdom on how to obtain wealth. God is not opposed to His children having wealth. On the contrary. He wants to lavish us with blessings, but our heart must be right, or it is all wasted. God's purpose in blessing us is so we can bless others.

We often make the mistake of thinking that God's law of reciprocity begins with God blessing us with abundance so we can bless others. He does bless us so we can be a blessing to others, but God's Word clearly states that we are to give and then it will be given to us. We must keep in mind that if we give little, our blessing will be small. If we give much, God will bless us abundantly. We might be surprised that "little" and "much" have nothing to do with how much we have or don't have. Let's look at two examples from scripture.

> Many who were rich gave much, but they gave out of their abundance. The widow appeared to give little, but she gave all she had, out of her poverty. Jesus said she gave more than anyone because she gave all she had, her whole livelihood. (Mark 12:41-44)

> The rich man, clothed in purple and fine linen, fared sumptuously every day as he had an overabundance of wealth and provision. Lazarus, the beggar, was willing to accept the crumbs which fell from the rich man's table. (Luke 16:19-22)

The passages above are not about how much we have, it's about the attitude of our heart. It's about faith and unbelief. Our heart attitude is reflected in every area of our lives. It is revealed in our giving and also in how we treat others.

In James 5:4-6, we see the manifestations of a heart focused on getting rather than giving:

We hold back employee wages by fraud.
We live on earth in pleasure and indulgence.
We have fattened our heart.
We condemn and murder the just.

It is easy to be drawn into the lure and seduction of gaining wealth. We must guard our heart and keep our attitude in check concerning wealth. We must also cultivate and maintain a heart of giving, and in so doing, we open the door to God's abundant blessing in our lives.

# ADDITIONAL SCRIPTURE

Genesis 13:2

Exodus 12:35-36

Job 42:10-12

Psalm 49

Psalm 105:37

Matthew 19:16-22

Mark 12:41-44

Luke 12:15, 21

Luke 16:19-22

## PRAYER

Father, give me wisdom to be a good steward of all you have given me
so I am able to bless others. In all I do, let it be solely for Your glory.

Amen.

## Study Questions

**Read James 5:1**

1.  Who is specifically included in this invitation?

2.  What are they invited to do?

3.  What is coming to them?

4.  Explain your answer to question 3.

# JOURNAL

Do the questions or scripture reading from today stir your spirit or emotions in any way?

Is there an area in your life or in your faith that needs a deeper look?

# Study Questions

If we only read James 5:1, we would assume having wealth is bad. Let's look at scripture that helps us have God's full perspective on wealth and possessions.

**Read Exodus 12:35-36**

1.  Who is asking for material blessing? Who told them to ask? Whom did they ask to bless them?

2.  List the items requested.

**Read Psalm 105:37**

3.  Who was the true initiator of their request? Did he grant their request?

4.  What added blessing is stated?

---
### PERSONAL

Can you describe a time when you knew God was blessing you through others?
Use the Journal section to record your answer.

---

# JOURNAL

Do the questions or scripture reading from today stir your spirit or emotions in any way?

Is there an area in your life or in your faith that needs a deeper look?

## Study Questions

**Read Genesis 13:2**

1. How is Abram described?

**Read Job 42:10-12**

2. Who is receiving blessing from the Lord?

3. Describe the blessing. Is there an amount mentioned?

4. Who did God prompt to add to Job's blessing? What did they give?

---

### CHALLENGE

**Read Job 42:13-17**

Describe the ways in which God
further blessed Job.

---

# JOURNAL

Do the questions or scripture reading from today stir your spirit or emotions in any way?
Is there an area in your life or in your faith that needs a deeper look?

## *Study Questions*

**Read Psalm 49.**

This passage clearly illustrates that having wealth is not the problem but a wrong attitude toward wealth causes problems.

1.  Which verses describe the futility of trusting in wealth?

2.  In verse 10, what happens to our wealth when we die? In verse 17, can we take our wealth with us when we die?

3.  What should believers consider true wealth?

# JOURNAL

Do the questions or scripture reading from today stir your spirit or emotions in any way?

Is there an area in your life or in your faith that needs a deeper look?

---- D A Y 5 ----
## *Study Questions*

**Read Matthew 19:16-22**

1. What question does the rich young ruler ask Jesus? How did Jesus answer?

2. How did the rich young ruler respond to Jesus' answer? What do you think Jesus was trying to reveal?

3. In verse 21, what was Jesus' final instruction to the young man?

4. In verse 22, describe the emotional response of the young man. What was revealed about the young man's heart attitude?

---

**CHALLENGE**

**Read Luke 12:15, 20**

In the Journal section,
describe the warnings given.

---

# JOURNAL

Do the questions or scripture reading from today stir your spirit or emotions in any way?

Is there an area in your life or in your faith that needs a deeper look?

## DAY 6
### Study Questions

**Read Mark 12:41-44**

**Read Luke 16:19-22**

1.  Name the people spoken of in both scriptures referenced above.

2.  Describe the heart attitude of each.

3.  Do you think God is concerned with how much we give? Why or why not?

4.  Which is more important to God – the act of giving or the heart attitude of the giver?

---

**CHALLENGE**

Is it possible to out-give God?
Write your answer in the Journal section.

---

Let's examine our hearts and look for opportunities to bless others!

# JOURNAL

Do the questions or scripture reading from today stir your spirit or emotions in any way?

Is there an area in your life or in your faith that needs a deeper look?

WE ARE TO

## plant seeds of God's Word

INTO THE CULTIVATED
SOIL OF THE HEARTS
OF OTHERS AND
TRUST GOD TO
PROVIDE WHAT IS
NECESSARY FOR THE
HARVEST OF SOULS.

# Faith and Christ's Return

*"Therefore be patient, brethren, until the coming of the Lord. See how the farmer waits for the precious fruit of the earth, waiting patiently for it until it receives the early and latter rain. You also be patient. Establish your hearts, for the coming of the Lord is at hand.*

*"Do not grumble against one another, brethren, lest you be condemned. Behold, the Judge is standing at the door! My brethren, take the prophets, who spoke in the name of the Lord, as an example of suffering and patience. Indeed we count them blessed who endure. You have heard of the perseverance of Job and seen the end intended by the Lord—that the Lord is very compassionate and merciful.*

*"But above all, my brethren, do not swear, either by heaven or by earth or with any other oath. But let your 'Yes' be 'Yes,' and your 'No,' 'No,' lest you fall into judgment."*

James 5:7-12

Patience is a virtue. That's what we have always heard. The natural response would be to ask for patience, but there is a warning from others not to ask for patience, because trials are what cultivate patience in our lives.

At this point, we find ourselves with a little conundrum – to ask or not to ask, that is the question; or is it? Trials will sweep through our lives whether or not we ask for patience. The proper response to trials is to allow God to work patience and many other qualities into our character.

In this passage we are commanded to be patient until the coming of the Lord. The example is given of a farmer waiting for his crop to grow and understanding that he has no control over what is needed to bring forth a harvest, which is the early and latter rain. We would be wise to consider the process of farming so we might better understand the need for patience as we await the coming of the Lord.

A good harvest doesn't just happen. There is an order to the process before the expectation of a harvest can be realized. The process begins with the preparation of the soil. It must be tilled and rows prepared. Then seeds are planted, watered, and fertilized. These are some of the things the farmer must do, and then he must wait and believe God will provide that over which the farmer has no control – the early and latter rain.

Like the farmer, we are to plant seeds of the Word into the cultivated soil of the hearts of others. We must water, fertilize and then trust God to provide what is necessary for the harvest of souls. Some will plant and some will water, but God gives the increase. This is the work to be done as we wait for the second coming of the Lord. I thank and praise God that He has left us with instructions as to the manner in which we await His glorious return.

Be patient like the farmer as we trust God's provision.

Establish our heart – for the coming of the Lord is near.

Do not grumble against one another.

Look to the example of the prophets.

Do not swear, by heaven or earth, or any other oath.

We are living in exciting times as we await the return of our Lord, Jesus Christ. Let's be diligent to follow the scripture so the Lord will say, "Well done, thou good and faithful servant!"

---

**PRAYER**

Father, as we await the second coming of our Lord, Jesus Christ,
make me keenly aware of those who need seeds of faith planted in their lives.
Go before me and prepare the soil of their heart to receive the seed of Your Word.
Send those after me to water the seeds and reap the harvest for Your kingdom.
Amen.

## Study Questions

**Read James 5:7**

1. What are we commanded to do?

2. Define patience.

3. What example is given?

4. Should we sit around doing nothing as we wait for the Lord?

---

### CHALLENGE

In the Journal section, describe
the impact of the early and
latter rain on farming.

---

# JOURNAL

Do the questions or scripture reading from today stir your spirit or emotions in any way?
Is there an area in your life or in your faith that needs a deeper look?

## Study Questions

**Read James 5:8**

1. What two things are we commanded to do?

2. Why are we commanded to do these things?

---

### PERSONAL

Are you excited for the coming of the Lord?

Why or why not?

Are you prepared for the coming of the Lord?

Why or why not?

What must you do to be prepared?

---

# JOURNAL

Do the questions or scripture reading from today stir your spirit or emotions in any way?

Is there an area in your life or in your faith that needs a deeper look?

## Study Questions

**Read James 5:9**

1.  What are we commanded?

2.  Is there a warning? If yes, what is it?

3.  Who is standing at the door? Describe the responsibility of this person.

4.  To whom does this verse ultimately refer? Support your answer with scripture references.

# JOURNAL

Do the questions or scripture reading from today stir your spirit or emotions in any way?

Is there an area in your life or in your faith that needs a deeper look?

## Study Questions

**Read James 5:10**

1. To whom are we to look as an example?

2. What was their purpose?

3. Whom did they represent?

4. Of what were they an example?

# JOURNAL

Do the questions or scripture reading from today stir your spirit or emotions in any way?

Is there an area in your life or in your faith that needs a deeper look?

## Study Questions

**Read James 5:11**

1. Who is counted as blessed?

2. Who is cited as an example from scripture?

3. How is he described?

4. Name two character traits of God.

---

### CHALLENGE

From Job 42:10-13, describe the end result of Job's faith through testing.

---

# JOURNAL

Do the questions or scripture reading from today stir your spirit or emotions in any way?
Is there an area in your life or in your faith that needs a deeper look?

## Study Questions

**Read James 5:12**

1. What does James warn against?

2. Why is this so important?

3. What are we commanded to do?

4. What is the consequence of disobedience to this command?

---

### PERSONAL

Is there anything you need to correct in your life so
you are in alignment with God's Word?
Use the Journal section to invite God into this area of your life.

---

# JOURNAL

Do the questions or scripture reading from today stir your spirit or emotions in any way?

Is there an area in your life or in your faith that needs a deeper look?

GOD'S WORD TELLS US TO
STAND AND PRAY.

*Every victory is won on the Battlefield of Prayer.*

# Faith in Action

*"Is anyone among you suffering? Let him pray. Is anyone cheerful? Let him sing psalms. Is anyone among you sick? Let him call for the elders of the church, and let them pray over him, anointing him with oil in the name of the Lord. And the prayer of faith will save the sick, and the Lord will raise him up. And if he has committed sins, he will be forgiven. Confess your trespasses to one another, and pray for one another, that you may be healed. The effective, fervent prayer of a righteous man avails much. Elijah was a man with a nature like ours, and he prayed earnestly that it would not rain; and it did not rain on the land for three years and six months. And he prayed again, and the heaven gave rain, and the earth produced its fruit.*

*"Brethren, if anyone among you wanders from the truth, and someone turns him back, let him know that he who turns a sinner from the error of his way will save a soul from death and cover a multitude of sins."*

James 5:13-20

As believers in Christ, we have everything we need to live victoriously. When we place our faith in Christ, we are given the Holy Spirit who leads and guides us into all truth. He is our comfort, counsel, and gives us wisdom. The Holy Spirit not only teaches us to pray but He intercedes for us when we don't know what to pray. God has provided armor for us which includes everything we need to defend ourselves against the attacks of the enemy. He has also provided one offensive weapon – the sword of the Spirit, which is the Word of God. After putting on the armor, God's Word tells us to stand and pray. Every victory is won on the battlefield of prayer.

In this passage above, James taught that the one who is suffering is to pray. Anyone who is cheerful is to sing psalms. If anyone is sick, they are to call the elders of the church to pray over them and anoint them with oil in Jesus' name. God has provided a formula for us to follow, but do we apply the formula? James has not left anything to guesswork.

| For those who are suffering | Pray |
| For those who are cheerful | Sing psalms |
| For those who are sick | Call for reinforcements. Have them pray and anoint with oil, specifically in Jesus' name. The oil represents the Holy Spirit- the presence of God. |

Then Jesus includes a great promise:

The prayer of faith will save the sick.
The Lord will raise him up and restore his health.
Sins will be forgiven, which is spiritual healing.

The Lord brings total healing – physical and spiritual – all because a prayer of faith was raised to the One who hears and answers our prayers.

What is a prayer of faith? It is a prayer of specific requests with the expectation God will answer favorably. Not that He **can** do what we have asked, but that He **will** do what we have asked.

As I write this, I realize there are those who have prayed a prayer of faith on behalf of others but did not receive the desired answer. The prayer of faith includes a willingness to accept God's answer as being best for the person for whom we are praying. Not my will, but God's will be done. We are praying with limited knowledge to the One who knows all things. He is trustworthy.

James adds to the formula for healing to:

Confess our trespasses to one another, and
Pray with each other, and
Be compassionate toward one another.

In NO WAY are we to judge others.

With this formula, another promise is included – the effective, fervent prayer of a righteous man accomplishes much. How can we pray effectively? By praying God's Word back to Him. He honors His Word. Once we know what to pray, we are to pray passionately. We cannot and must not enter prayer casually. In James 5:17, Elijah is given as an example. He was a man with a sin nature, yet he prayed, and God answered. Elijah prayed very specifically, believing God would both hear and answer. His faith was rewarded when God answered his prayer.

James 5:19-20 reminds us that occasionally our faith in God will require confrontation. This word of instruction pertains to fellow believers and, specifically, when a fellow believer departs from the truth of God's Word. This is an opportunity to confront with the express purpose of saving and restoring. In Galatians 6:1, God gives instructions to the one who would confront. He says it is to be done in a spirit of gentleness, and we are to be mindful of the fact that the one who is confronting could also be tempted.

We must remain mindful that ALL things must be done in faith; faith in God alone.

## ADDITIONAL SCRIPTURE

1 Kings 17:1; 18:1

1 Chronicles 28:9

Mark 6:13

Romans 8:26-27

Galatians 6:1

Ephesians 6:10-18

1 John 5:14

## PRAYER

Father, teach me to pray Your Word effectively and passionately.
Demonstrate Your power as I pray on behalf of others so my faith will be
strengthened to continue in prayer for all the needs of those around me.
Remind me daily that the true effectiveness of my prayer is NOT that I pray,
but that You hear and answer in Your time and in Your way.
Amen.

# *Study Questions*

**Read James 5:13-14**

1. What conditions are listed? (i.e. suffering)

2. List the prescribed treatment for each condition. (i.e. suffering – pray)

3. When illness strikes, what are we instructed to do?

4. Describe the process used by the elders of the church.

# JOURNAL

Do the questions or scripture reading from today stir your spirit or emotions in any way?
Is there an area in your life or in your faith that needs a deeper look?

## Study Questions

**Read Mark 6:13**

1.  Describe the challenges the disciples faced.

2.  How were the challenges addressed?

3.  What was the result?

4.  What did the apostles need to possess in order to do these miracles?

# JOURNAL

Do the questions or scripture reading from today stir your spirit or emotions in any way?

Is there an area in your life or in your faith that needs a deeper look?

## DAY 3
### *Study Questions*

**Read James 5:15-16**

1.  Describe the type of prayer mentioned.

2.  List the results promised from this type of prayer.

3.  Define trespasses. What are we supposed to do with our trespasses? What should be done afterward?

4.  Define effective. Define fervent. Define avail.

---

### PERSONAL

Does having a clearer understanding of how we should pray
cause a desire to make changes in your personal prayer time?
Use the Journal section to express changes you would
like to make. Sign and date the page.

---

# JOURNAL

Do the questions or scripture reading from today stir your spirit or emotions in any way?
Is there an area in your life or in your faith that needs a deeper look?

# Study Questions

**Read Romans 8:26-27**

1.  Who helps us? Why is His help necessary?

2.  Describe how He makes intercession for us.

**Read 1 Chronicles 28:9**

3.  Who searches the hearts? How does He make intercession for believers?

**Read 1 John 5:14**

4.  What assurance are we given according to this passage?

# JOURNAL

Do the questions or scripture reading from today stir your spirit or emotions in any way?

Is there an area in your life or in your faith that needs a deeper look?

# Study Questions

For background information about Elijah, **read 1 Kings 18**

**Read James 5:17-18** and answer the following questions:

1. Describe Elijah.

2. Describe Elijah's attitude in prayer.

3. Tell what he prayed for specifically.

4. Does Elijah's prayer reflect the kind of prayer described in this verse?

---

### PERSONAL

The story found in 1 Kings 18 is a beautiful example
of God's power through prayer.
Have you prayed for something with the same intensity as Elijah in these passages?
How does this encourage you in your prayer life?

Do the questions or scripture reading from today stir your spirit or emotions in any way?

Is there an area in your life or in your faith that needs a deeper look?

## Study Questions

**Read James 5:19-20**

1. Describe the situation.

2. What is the desired outcome from such a confrontation?

**Read Galatians 6:1**

3. In what spirit should one confront another?

4. What caution is given?

---

### PRAYER

Father, open my eyes to see the prayer needs around me.

Thank you that I am righteous because of the blood of Jesus Christ.

Engage my heart to pray effectively and passionately.

May my prayers accomplish much, not because of who I am

but because of Your faithfulness.

Amen.

# JOURNAL

Do the questions or scripture reading from today stir your spirit or emotions in any way?

Is there an area in your life or in your faith that needs a deeper look?

# A CLOSING WORD TO THE READER

When I entered into a personal relationship with Christ, I asked Him for four things. I told Him I wanted to know Him intimately (who He is in MY life), I asked Him to teach me how to pray effectively, I wanted to be able to sing praise to Him, and I wanted to serve Him. More than anything I wanted to know how to pray! I was raised in a denomination that provided prayers already written by other people and that is the only way I knew how to pray. They were beautiful prayers, but I wanted to pray to God from my own heart.

He certainly answered that heartfelt prayer and taught me to pray His Word, which is the most effective way to pray. The reason is that He does not just speak words, He IS His Word, and He can't deny Himself.

I have been able to find prayers and promises to pray for all my needs, but that is not to say He answers all my prayers when or how I would like them to be answered. As a matter of fact, He seldom answers according to my timing. He is God and I am not. He knows what is best for me and He always desires my highest good. His timing is perfect – He is never late, never early, He is always on time.

The entire book of James is powerful for life and living, but James 5:16 is critical for the life of a believer and the Christian community. Instructions are given in this verse concerning prayer:

> Confess your trespasses to one another.
> Pray for one another – that you may be healed.

The last part of this verse describes the kind of prayer that makes a difference. It says the effective, fervent prayer of a righteous man avails much. We know we are righteous because we are under the blood of Jesus Christ, so we are covered there, but are we praying fervently (passionately)? I believe the reason most Christians don't pray passionately is because they can't feel the pain or sense of urgency of the one who needs prayer.

The word, effectively, begs the question - how do we pray effectively? I can always tell by someone's prayer how much time they spend in the Word. You see, the more time we spend in God's Word, the more powerful and effective our prayers become. The Bible says when we ask according to God's will, it will be done for us. Knowing God's Word teaches us how to pray according to His will because it teaches us to know Him. We learn His character, what pleases and displeases Him, His ways, and most importantly, His heart toward us who believe.

As previously stated, the Bible contains many prayers and promises for us to use as templates for prayer or to just pray and claim outright. I am including some of those prayers for your convenience, but our resource for prayer in the Bible is inexhaustible. As you study, write meaningful verses and promises you can use in your prayer time. Of utmost importance is setting aside time for prayer. It requires discipline and must be intentional.

Prayer is essential for effecting change in our personal lives, our families, churches, communities, our nation, and our world. Throughout history, prayer has played a part in shaping our world, but now more than ever we need to put on the armor of God, take up our sword (the Word of God), and pray. I believe we are never more powerful than when we fall on our knees in prayer to our Almighty God.

Let's unite our hearts in effective prayer and see what God can do!

# PRAYERS FROM THE BIBLE

Please allow me to introduce some of the powerful prayers found in the Word. This is not an exhaustive list of prayers found in the Bible. There are many more!

*"That the God of our Lord Jesus Christ, the Father of glory, may give to you the spirit of wisdom and revelation in the knowledge of Him, the eyes of your understanding being enlightened; that you may know what is the hope of His calling, what are the riches of the glory of His inheritance in the saints."* (Ephesians 1:17-18)

*"That He would grant you, according to the riches of His glory, to be strengthened with might through His Spirit in the inner man, that Christ may dwell in your hearts through faith; that you, being rooted and grounded in love, may be able to comprehend with all the saints what is the width and length and depth and height – to know the love of Christ which passes knowledge; that you may be filled with all the fullness of God."* (Ephesians 3:16-19)

*"And this I pray, that your love may abound still more and more in knowledge and all discernment, that you may approve the things that are excellent, that you may be sincere and without offense till the day of Christ, being filled with the fruits of righteousness which are by Jesus Christ, to the glory and praise of God."* (Philippians 1:9-11)

*"For this reason we also, since the day we heard it, do not cease to pray for you, and to ask that you may be filled with the knowledge of His will in all wisdom and spiritual understanding; that you may walk worthy of the Lord, fully pleasing Him being fruitful in every good work and increasing in the knowledge of God; strengthened with all might according to His glorious power, for all patience and longsuffering with joy; giving thanks to the Father who has qualified us to be partakers of the inheritance of the saints in the light."* (Colossians 1:8-12)

*"And may the Lord make you increase and abound in love to one another and to all, just as we do to you, so that He may establish your hearts blameless in holiness before our God and Father at the coming of our Lord Jesus Christ with all His saints."* (1 Thessalonians 3:12-13)

*"Now may the Lord Jesus Christ Himself and our God and Father, who has loved us and given us everlasting consolation and good hope by grace, comfort your hearts and establish you in every good word and work."* (2 Thessalonians 2:16)

*"Lord, it is nothing for You to help, whether with many or with those who have no power; help us, O Lord our God, for we rest on you, and in Your name we go against this multitude. O lord, You are our God; do not let man prevail against You!"* (2 Chronicles 14:11)

"O our God, will You not judge them? For we have no power against this great multitude that is coming against us; nor do we know what to do, but our eyes are upon You." (2 Chronicles 20:12)

"Blessed be the name of God forever and ever, for wisdom and might are His. And He changes the times and the seasons; He removes kings and raises up kings; He gives wisdom to the wise and knowledge to those who have understanding. He reveals deep and secret things; He knows what is in the darkness, and light dwells with Him. I thank You and praise You, O God of my fathers; You have given me wisdom and might, and have now made known to me what we asked of You....." (Daniel 2:20-23)

"But may the God of all grace, who called us to His eternal glory by Christ Jesus, after you have suffered a while, perfect, establish, strengthen, and settle you. To Him be all the glory and the dominion forever and ever. Amen." (1Peter 5:10-11)

"Now may the God of peace who brought up our Lord Jesus from the dead, that great Shepherd of the sheep, through the blood of the everlasting covenant, may you complete in every good work to do His will, working in you what is well and pleasing in His sight, through Jesus Christ, to whom be glory forever and ever. Amen." (Hebrews 13:20-21)

"Now to Him who is able to keep you from stumbling, and to present you faultless before the presence of His glory with exceeding joy, to God our Savior, who alone is wise, be glory and majesty, dominion and power, both now and forever. Amen." (Jude 24-25)

"Oh, that You would bless me indeed, and enlarge my territory, that Your hand would be with me, and that You would keep me from evil, that I may not cause pain!" (1 Chronicles 4:10)

"I pray that you may prosper in all things and be in health, just as your soul prospers." (3 John 1:2)

"The Lord bless you and keep you; the Lord make His face shine upon you, and be gracious to you; the Lord lift up His countenance upon you, and give you peace." (Numbers 6:24-26)

# ACKNOWLEDGEMENTS

In truth, there are too many people to list who have inspired, encouraged, and mentored me so I will, for the purpose of this devotional, only list those related to this work.

First, I want to thank God for the experiences in my life, both good and bad, that have enabled me to have a deeper understanding of His Word, thus providing the material needed for this devotional.

While the inspiration came from God, the encouragement (push) came from my dear friend, Arlette Jeffries, who not only encouraged, but also helped in the architecture of this kind of devotional. She is the one who wisely said it needed to be something the reader would ponder for more than just a day.

Also critical to this book were the godly friends who painstakingly went through my rough manuscript and made corrections for me.

Not in any particular order:

Pearl Hodges
Sherry Baker
Arlette Jeffries
Gail Jones
My Pastor, Dr. Joe Worley

Special thanks to –

Julie Weeks for her words of encouragement and her patience in helping me with technology and related resources. Her help was invaluable.

Mary Ethel Eckard, my editor/publisher, for her expertise and wisdom in turning my manuscript into a published work! Words cannot express my gratitude!

My heart is filled with gratitude, and I am indebted to these siblings in Christ for helping me produce this devotional.

Blessings,
Karen

*"The Lord bless you and keep you;*
*the Lord make His face shine upon you,*
*and be gracious to you;*
*the Lord lift up His countenance upon you,*
*and give you peace."*

Numbers 6:24-26

# APPENDIX A
# The Plan of Salvation

*"For God so loved the world that He gave His only begotten Son that whoever believes in Him should not perish, but have everlasting life. For God did not send His Son into the world to condemn the world, but that the world through Him might be saved."*

John 3:16-17

The invitation to salvation in Jesus Christ is extended to all people.

**Why do we need to be saved?**

Romans 3:23 – *"For all have sinned and fall short of the glory of God."*

Romans 6:23 – *"For the payment for sin is death, but the gift of God is eternal life in Christ Jesus our Lord."*

Romans 5:8 – *"But God demonstrated His own love for us in that while we were still sinners, Christ died for us."*

**How can we be saved?**

Jesus offered Himself as the sinless sacrifice to atone for the sins of all people.

Ephesians 2:8-9 – *"For by grace you have been saved through faith, and that not of yourselves; it is the gift of God, not by works lest anyone should boast."*

Romans 10:9-10 – *"That if you confess with your mouth the Lord Jesus and believe in your heart that God has raised Him from the dead, you will be saved. For with the heart one believes unto righteousness and with the mouth confession is made to salvation."*

**To receive salvation we must:**

1. Acknowledge we are sinners
2. Believe in our heart that Jesus paid the price for our sins through His death on the cross.
3. We must confess with our mouth that Jesus is Savior and Lord.

You can accomplish this by praying a simple prayer. I have written one below, but you can pray your own prayer as well.

**Prayer**

Father, I acknowledge that I am a sinner and I ask for Your forgiveness. I believe Jesus paid the price for my sins through His death on the cross and provided eternal life for all who believe in Him, through His resurrection from the dead. I surrender my whole heart to Jesus Christ as my Savior and my Lord. Amen.

Begotten:    to have born, brought forth[5]
Atone:        to make amends: to provide or serve as reparation or compensation for something unwelcome.

.....when it first entered English, atonement: "to reconcile" and suggested the restoration of a peaceful and harmonious state between people or groups.

These days the verb specifically implies addressing the damage (or disharmony) caused by one's own behavior.

i.e...our sin causes separation or disharmony between us and God the Father.[6]

Righteousness: The quality of being morally true or justifiable. In its deeper spiritual meaning, righteousness is the quality of being right in the eyes of God including character (nature), conscience (attitude), conduct (actions), and command (word). Righteousness is, therefore, based upon God's standard because He is the ultimate lawgiver. (Isaiah 33:22)

# NOTES

1   KJV dictionary AV1611.com

2   Fire insurance is a way of saying we have been rescued from spending eternity in hell. Many believers accept Christ as their Savior but do not take further steps to follow Him and grow in His teachings and likeness.

3   Cambridge Dictionary. Cambridge Press.

4   Max Lucado, *Grace for the Moment: Inspirational Thoughts for Each Day of the Year* (Nashville, TN.: Thomas Nelson), 255.

5   Source: biblestudytools.com

6   Source: Merriam Webster Dictionary

# JOURNAL

# JOURNAL

# JOURNAL

# JOURNAL

# JOURNAL

# JOURNAL

# JOURNAL

# JOURNAL

# JOURNAL

www.ingramcontent.com/pod-product-compliance
Lightning Source LLC
Chambersburg PA
CBHW080836120626
46553CB00009B/2457